THE WORLD THE FLESH AND THE DEVIL

THE
WORLD
THE
FLESH
AND THE
DEVIL

JIMMY SWAGGART

JIMMY SWAGGART MINISTRIES
P.O. Box 262550 | Baton Rouge, Louisiana 70826-2550
Website: www.jsm.org | Email: info@jsm.org | Phone: 225.768.7000

ISBN 978-1-941403-23-5

09-130 | COPYRIGHT © 2015 Jimmy Swaggart Ministries®

15 16 17 18 19 20 21 22 23 / DP / 10 9 8 7 6 5 4 3 2 1

iv

TABLE OF CONTENTS

THE
WORLD
THE
FLESH
AND THE
DEVIL

INTRODUCTION

INTRODUCTION

THE EARLY CHURCH COINED a phrase that I think has not been improved upon as it regards our everyday living for God. It is, *"the world, the flesh, and the Devil."* Those are the antagonists to the child of God.

THE WORLD

"Love not the world, neither the things that are in the world. If any man love the world, the love of the Father is not in him" (I Jn. 2:15).

The *"world"* spoken of here by John pertains to the ordered system of which Satan is the head.

God the Father will not share with the world the love that must go exclusively to Him. This is one of the greatest conflicts as it regards the child of God — the world.

Satan is the god of this present world (II Cor. 4:4). He is also the *"prince of this world"* (Jn. 12:31). This means that he is the god or prince of the system of this world, which is not the friend of the child of God. It's something about which we must be careful on a constant basis. We are in the world but not of the world.

THE FLESH

What is the flesh?

As Paul used the word, it speaks of that which is indigenous to man. In other words, it is our education, motivation, talent, personal ability, personal strength, will power, etc.

Paul said: *"For they who are after the flesh do mind the things of the flesh; but they who are after the Spirit the things of the Spirit"* (Rom. 8:5).

The flesh refers to believers trying to live for the Lord by means other than faith in Christ and the Cross. Those who place their faith in Christ and the Cross must do so exclusively, which means that they are doing what the Holy Spirit desires. This alone can bring victory.

Paul also bluntly said, *"So then they who are in the flesh cannot please God"* (Rom. 8:8). Once again, this means that the believer tries to live for God on a daily basis by means other than Christ and what Christ did for us at the Cross.

Paul also said, *"I am crucified with Christ: nevertheless I live; yet not I, but Christ lives in me: and the life which I now live in the flesh I live by the faith of the Son of God, who loved me, and gave Himself for me"* (Gal. 2:20).

When Paul said, *"And the life which I now live in the flesh,"* he meant that we are human beings, and though we are in the flesh, our life and living are not by the flesh. That's why he said *"yet not I."* These are probably the three words that Christians need to learn more than anything else. It is *"not I, but Christ who lives in me."*

The flesh is without a doubt the greatest nemesis and the greatest hindrance faced by the child of God. Let us say it again: *"We are in the flesh, but we are not of the flesh."*

The believer is to understand that what we are facing in the spirit world, and I speak of the powers of darkness, are far beyond our ability to cope as it regards the flesh. That's what makes humanistic psychology so foolish.

We can live this life if we do it God's way, and His way is the Cross. If our faith is exclusively in Christ and the Cross, the Holy Spirit, who is God, and who can do anything, will then work mightily on our behalf. If we resort to the flesh, this greatly hinders the Holy Spirit, with Him then unable to function as He desires to do so. It is the business of the Holy Spirit to rid our lives of all sin and of all dependence on the flesh. With that being accomplished, the Holy Spirit will work grandly on our behalf, doing for us what only He can do. This is God's way, and His only way. Abiding by that particular *"way,"* we can be victorious in every capacity. But if we try to live this life by the means of the flesh, no matter how sincere we are and no matter the effort put forth, we will fail, and fail miserably.

THE DEVIL

"Be sober, be vigilant; because your adversary the Devil, as a roaring lion, walks about, seeking whom he may devour: Whom resist steadfast in the faith, knowing that the same afflictions are accomplished in your brethren who are in the world" (I Pet. 5:8-9).

Satan heads up the kingdom of darkness and, of course, is greatly opposed to every believer.

There is one way, and only one way, that we can defeat him and live this life as it should be lived. It is by our faith in Christ and the Cross (Rom. 6:1-14; 8:1-11; I Cor. 1:17-18, 23; 2:2; Gal. 6:14).

Paul said: *"Blotting out the handwriting of ordinances that was against us, which was contrary to us, and took it out of the way, nailing it to His Cross; and having spoiled principalities and powers, He made a show of them openly, triumphing over them in it"* (Col. 2:14-15).

The reason that Satan hates the Cross as he does is because it was there that he was totally defeated.

How was he defeated?

Sin is that which gives Satan the legal right to hold man captive. However, Jesus atoned for all sin, past, present, and future — at least for all who will believe — by the giving of Himself as a perfect sacrifice on the Cross, which satisfied the demands of a thrice-holy God.

WE WRESTLE NOT AGAINST FLESH AND BLOOD

Paul said, *"Put on the whole armor of God, that you may be able to stand against the wiles of the Devil. For we wrestle not against flesh and blood, but against principalities, against powers, against the rulers of the darkness of this world, against spiritual wickedness in high places"* (Eph. 6:11-12).

This is the reason that all man-devised practices will not work as it regards Satan. If we do this thing God's way, which way is the Cross, we will then walk in victory. Otherwise, we will walk in defeat. As we have said, Satan cannot stand the Cross, and for all the obvious reasons.

GOD'S WAY

- Jesus Christ is the source of all things we receive from God (Rom. 6:1-14; Jn. 1:1-3, 14, 29).
- The Cross of Christ is the means, and the only means, by which all of these wonderful things are given to us (Col. 2:10-15).
- With Jesus as our source and the Cross as our means, our faith must then be placed exclusively in Christ and the Cross. In fact, the entirety of the story of the Bible is *"Jesus Christ and Him crucified."* Our faith must not be in other things but always in Christ and what He has done for us at the Cross (I Cor. 1:17-18, 23; 2:2; Gal., Chpt. 5; 6:14).
- With Christ as our source, the Cross as our means, and our faith firmly planted and maintained in Christ and the Cross, the Holy Spirit (who works exclusively within the parameters of the finished work of Christ) will then work mightily on our behalf. He is God, and there is nothing impossible for Him (Rom. 8:1-11; Eph. 2:13-18).

In abbreviated form, what I have given you is the way we have victory over the world, the flesh, and the Devil.

This book will give us Old Testament examples, types, and shadows in picture form that will explain that of which we speak. In other words, it makes it easier to understand.

The Old Testament is written in the form of a television set, while the New Testament is written in the form of a computer.

EXAMPLES

Paul said, *"Now these things were our examples, to the intent we should not lust after evil things, as they also lusted.*

"Neither be you idolaters, as were some of them; as it is written, The people sat down to eat and drink, and rose up to play.

"Neither let us commit fornication, as some of them committed, and fell in one day three and twenty thousand.

"Neither let us tempt Christ, as some of them also tempted, and were destroyed of serpents.

"Neither murmur you, as some of them also murmured, and were destroyed of the destroyer.

"Now all these things happened unto them for examples: and they are written for our admonition, upon whom the ends of the world are come" (I Cor. 10:6-11).

So, I pray that we will make the examples so clear and so obvious that these things which are intended by the Holy Spirit will be adequately learned. Considering that it is the

single most important material that any believer could grasp
and understand, it is imperative that it be taught correctly and
that it be learned correctly. Our victory or the lack thereof is
dependent on the instruction given.

> *I have entered the valley of blessing so sweet,*
> *And Jesus abides with me there,*
> *And His Spirit and blood make my cleansing complete,*
> *And His perfect love casts out fear.*
>
> *There is peace in the valley of blessing so sweet.*
> *And plenty the land does impart;*
> *And there's rest for the weary, worn traveler's feet,*
> *And joy for the sorrowing heart.*
>
> *There is love in the valley of blessing so sweet.*
> *Such as none but the blood-washed may feel,*
> *When heaven comes down redeemed spirits to greet,*
> *And Christ sets His covenant seal.*
>
> *There's a song in the valley of blessing so sweet,*
> *And angels would fain join the strain,*
> *As with rapturous praises we bow at His feet,*
> *Crying, Worthy the Lamb that was slain!*

THE WORLD THE FLESH AND THE DEVIL

THE LORD SHOWED HIM A TREE

THE LORD SHOWED HIM A TREE

"THEN SANG MOSES AND the children of Israel this song unto the Lord, and spoke, saying, I will sing unto the Lord, for He has triumphed gloriously: the horse and his rider has He thrown into the sea" (Ex. 15:1).

Moses began and ended his wilderness life with a song. That of Deuteronomy, Chapter 32, is the one referred to in Revelation 15:3. There was no singing in Egypt; there was groaning. Singing only follows redemption.

The song portrayed in Chapter 15 of Exodus is the oldest song of praise in existence. The greatest poets unite in admiration of its surpassing beauty and sublimity. It is a song of praise. Its theme is Jehovah Jesus, one might say. It praises Him for His destruction of the enemy. It begins with redemption and ends with glory.

There were two companies of singers — one formed of men, led by Moses, the other of women, led by Miriam. She and her choir *"answered the men."* This is the first of the 10 songs of praise recorded in the Bible; the last is Revelation 14:3.

"Self" is absent from this song. It is all about Jehovah and His power to save.

I WILL SING UNTO THE LORD

The first song recorded in the Bible is that of Lamech, but it certainly is not of the Lord, being a song that glorifies man's inhumanity to his fellow man (Gen. 4:23-24).

This song recorded in Exodus, Chapter 15, celebrates the deliverance of the children of Israel from Egyptian bondage and glorifies the Lord who has done the delivering. It is the first song of praise and redemption simply because redemption had been carried out in type. The song was accompanied by tens of thousands of tambourines, i.e., *"timbrels,"* which were, no doubt, of every size and description. As well, tens of thousands of Israelite women — seemingly both young and old — danced before the Lord to the accompaniment of the musical instruments and the singing as they gave praise to the Lord for His great deliverance from Egyptian bondage. Consequently, as it is recorded in the Word of God, Moses wrote the very first gospel song, so to speak. He also wrote the very first psalm (Psalm 90). More than likely, he also wrote Psalm 91.

So, the very first thing we find after the salvation and redemption of the children of Israel is rejoicing. No wonder!

REJOICING

When a person comes to Christ (any person), joy fills the heart simply because the enmity between them and God, which was caused by sin, has now been removed due to the shed blood of Christ being applied to the heart and life. This is all done by faith (Jn. 3:16; Eph. 2:8-9). So, this which the children of Israel did on the far shore of the Red Sea portrays the joy of the heart and the joy of the soul for what the Lord has done. It is the only true joy there is and the only true rejoicing there is.

This doesn't mean that every new convert, or every Christian for that matter, has to sing and dance before the Lord, but it definitely does mean that there will be a rejoicing heart. That goes with salvation, and I really cannot see how in the world that anyone could come to Christ — which means to be *"born again,"* which means that they are now a new creation in Christ Jesus — and not have a rejoicing heart.

CHRISTIANITY

As well, we are told that there are seven major religions in the world. Although not a religion, but rather a relationship with Christ, still, Christianity is put in that category. It is the only one of the seven that has a songbook because it is the only one of the seven that has anything to sing about.

To show the reader how important the right kind of music and singing is as it regards the worship of the Lord, we need only to look at the book of Psalms, which is the largest book in the Bible. This tells us what the Holy Spirit thinks of worship, and it tells us how that the greatest degree of worship is found in music and singing. There are certainly other ways to worship God, but I think that the greatest way of all, or possibly that which the Holy Spirit uses more than all, is music and singing.

MUSIC

Music, as devised by the Lord, is made up of rhythm, melody, and harmony. If any one of those three is hindered, continuity is destroyed, and it becomes virtually impossible to worship the Lord by such music. So-called modern contemporary Christian music falls into that category. It may be referred to as *"Christian,"* but it is not Christian. While the flesh may respond to such music, it is impossible for the spirit of the individual to do so.

Most of these so-called Christian rock entertainers, and that's what they are, look to the mainstream rockers as their examples, which, to be frank, is an abomination. The tragedy is, pastors will shepherd their young people into these so-called concerts, which have absolutely no spirituality, at least as it regards the Lord. In fact, to be blunt, clear, and plain, this particular type of music is of Satan. It's not of God, it has never been of God, and it is abominable to even claim that it is. Pastors who promote such stuff are going to answer to God for the souls of the young people under their charge.

INSPIRATION!

As we have already alluded, most of these so-called Christian groups get their inspiration from their worldly counterparts. Now, think about that for a moment, please! How in the world can someone be inspired by those who are controlled by demon spirits and still claim that what they're doing is of the Lord? In fact, such is an abomination before the Lord.

To be frank, the name of that game is money. So-called Christian rock is to the secular rock music scene as methadone is to the drug scene.

Radio stations that refer to themselves as Christian and play that type of music are actually promoting the Devil. Christian television shows that feature such fall into the same category. To be sure, the owners of such stations, the deejays, and the pastors of churches who promote this stuff, or even who place their seal of approval on it, once again, are going to answer to God, and the answer is not going to be very favorable.

Exactly as secular rock music, all of its promotion of drugs, illicit sex, alcohol, and murder contain a spirit of darkness that joins with the spirit of those who listen to such so-called music. It is the same identical thing with the so-called Christian rock. There is a bondage to such music exactly as there is to alcohol, drugs, gambling, and nicotine.

WIN THE YOUTH?

Win them to what?

Ten years ago, it was claimed that such music would win young people to Christ. What a ridiculous statement that is! People are brought to Christ not by using the raw ways of the world, or any ways of the world for that matter, but rather by the Holy Spirit. To be sure, He not only doesn't need the ways of the world, He absolutely rejects the ways of the world. So, anyone who would claim such a thing simply doesn't know the Bible and has no knowledge of the Lord per se.

However, most now are not even claiming that such is winning youth to Christ, but rather that it's *"good clean entertainment."* While it might be entertainment, it's definitely not good, and it's definitely not clean. To be frank, there are almost as many drugs sold or used at these Christian rock concerts as in the secular concerts.

That particular type of music, if it can be called music, certainly doesn't glorify God. To be frank, to even insinuate that it does is an insult to the Lord.

A PERSONAL EXPERIENCE

Some years ago, Frances and I were in Budapest, Hungary, in a particular church for a service. Not being able to speak or understand Hungarian, I had no idea of the words they were saying as it regarded the songs they were singing; however, I did recognize the melodies, and you could sense the presence of the Lord as the people were worshipping. While they sang in Hungarian, I sang the same song in English.

Just before the service was turned to me, they had a young man sing, who had just come from the United States. He got up and sang a particular song that he had learned in the states, which he had translated into Hungarian. It was one of the Christian rock songs. As stated, that particular music has no melody or harmony. As a result, the people just sat there and stared because there was nothing else they could do. As stated, it is impossible to worship with that type of music, and to be frank, who would want to try to worship with such being offered?

The people in the church little knew me, if at all, and I did not know them either. So, what I was seeing was not staged, but yet, was a perfect example of this of which I speak. As they sang the old songs of glory, they could worship the Lord simply because the songs were of the Lord. When the young man sang, presenting the garbage — and that's exactly what it was — that he had learned in the states, they could not worship simply because worship to such is impossible. Those who claim they can worship the Lord according to such simply do not know what worship actually is.

THE SPIRITUAL BAROMETER

One can pretty well judge the spiritual barometer of a church by the type of music that it promotes. The Spirit of the Lord will portray Himself in this particular category of worship as He does in nothing else. As stated, the book of Psalms is the largest book in the Bible, telling us what the Holy Spirit thinks of worship according to music and singing. If, in fact, I am correct about music being a spiritual barometer, then the churches in the United States are in sad shape indeed! There are exceptions, and thank God for those exceptions, but they are few and far between.

UNTO THE LORD

The song that Moses sang — along with the children of Israel — was evidently given to him by the Lord. Immediately, it glorified the Lord, speaking of the great victory that He had brought about for the children of Israel. It began that way, and it ended that way.

I was either 8 or 9 years of age; the exact year slips my mind. At any rate, I had just been saved and baptized with the Holy Spirit a short time earlier. On a particular night in question, while in church and observing the evangelist as he played the piano, the Lord put it into my heart to seek Him as it regarded the talent to play that particular instrument. I can remember sitting beside my dad, and all through the service, asking the Lord for this particular talent. I remember very vividly some of the things I said to Him.

Being just a child, I knew very little about sin, but I remember promising the Lord that if He would give me this talent, I would forever use it for His glory. I also remember saying that I would never play in a nightclub. That is about the limit that I had of things of the world at that particular time.

I can still see myself sitting beside my dad. I can see myself praying, and once or twice, my whispering to the Lord must have become obvious because my dad looked at me and shook his head as if to say, *"Be quiet."*

At any rate, I could hardly wait for the service to conclude. I had asked the Lord for this talent, and I believed in my heart with simple childlike faith that the Lord had heard me, and He would give me that for which I had asked.

THE PIANO

When the service ended, I very hesitantly walked up onto the small platform. Our church was very small, and the musical complement consisted only of an old upright piano.

To my recollection, I had never sat down on a piano stool in my life. So, for the first time, I sat down and put my fingers on the keys. Immediately, I began to make chords. I did not know what the chords were, but I did know the finger positions were right because it sounded right to my ear.

After the service, my dad asked me where I had learned those chords, for, evidently, he had heard me. I shook my head in the negative and replied that I had not learned them anywhere. Ignoring what I had said, he asked me if I had been up to my aunt's house, who had a piano, and if I had been playing her instrument.

"No," I replied!

He then asked, "Has Sister Culbreth (our pastor's wife, who was an excellent pianist) been showing you some chords?"

I again replied in the negative.

He then asked, "Well, have you been going to the church to practice?"

Once again, I replied "No!"

"Well, where did you learn those chords?" he asked.

I remember my reply as though this happened yesterday. I said, "I asked the Lord to give me the talent to play the piano, and I guess He has already started!"

I don't recall what he said then, but I do remember that he very much approved of my request.

A GIFT FROM THE LORD

Some may remonstrate by saying that musical talent runs in my family, and the Lord had nothing to do with what talent I do have. While it is certainly true that musical talent definitely runs in my family, with two of my cousins being quite prominent in the musical field, still, I believe that the Lord gave me the talent that I have. Along with the talent to play the piano, I believe He also gave me an understanding of music that glorifies His name. Whatever style I have was not copied from anyone. The Lord gave it to me exactly as it is. With our music, we have seen literally millions of people blessed, stirred, encouraged, and strengthened in the Lord. Of course, I give Him all the praise and all the glory.

In respect to what I've just said about the Lord giving me a knowledge of music which glorifies Him, that doesn't mean that for music to glorify the Lord, it has to be identical to the music that I play. That would be facetious, to say the least! But I definitely do believe that it will be somewhat similar.

Music is not neutral. It was originated by God. The Word of God tells us that when God created the Earth, *"the morn-*

ing stars (angels) *sang together, and all the sons of God shouted for joy"* (Job 38:4-7).

Once again, we go back to the book of Psalms and realize that in every one of the psalms and songs — for that's what the word *psalms* actually means — the Holy Spirit gave the words, and even gave instructions to the writers of some of the psalms as to what type of musical instrumentation should accompany the psalm. When we realize this, we should then understand just how important music and singing actually are as it regards the worship of the Lord.

Over the SonLife Radio Network and the SonLife Broadcasting Network, we play only music that originates at Family Worship Center. Concerning this, a man wrote me the other day and stated, "Brother Swaggart, thank you so much for putting the station in our city (he was speaking of a radio station owned by the ministry). You are teaching us how to worship."

I will confess that when I read his note, I was somewhat taken aback. But yet, after a moment, I realized that most churches have been so off track, regarding the worship of the Lord, for such a long time that they hardly know what true worship is anymore.

WORSHIP

I'm certainly not meaning that this applies to all churches, for it doesn't; however, I definitely do believe that it applies to most. As we've already stated, music is a barometer, I think, of the spirituality of the church. When the spirituality begins to go wrong, which means the pastor and people are veering away from the Word of God, it will tell first of all in the music that they produce. So, when I make statements about music, I am, at least to a certain extent, making statements in the realm of revelation from the Lord. In other words, I know somewhat of that of which I speak. That's at least one of the reasons I cannot stand to listen to modern so-called Christian rock, or whatever it is, which is nothing but a product of the flesh, and which only appeals to the flesh. Then I hear the voice of the Holy Spirit saying: *"So then they who are in the flesh cannot please God"* (Rom. 8:8).

That which we do as it regards anything done for the Lord, especially our worship as it regards music and singing, must glorify His name. As is portrayed to us here very clearly, this great song was sung by Moses and the children of Israel. I think we should conclude that the Holy Spirit would desire that we use this presentation as a foundation for our musical efforts. As we will see, the Lord is glorified throughout, with man glorified not at all.

THE LORD

"The LORD is my strength and song, and He is become my salvation: He is my God, and I will prepare Him an habitation; my father's God, and I will exalt Him" (Ex. 15:2).

The first phrase actually says in the Hebrew, *"My strength and song is Jah."* In fact, the name *Jah* had not previously been used. It is commonly regarded as an abbreviated form of Jehovah. It takes the place of *Jehovah* here probably because of the rhythm of the song. The *"salvation"* addressed here refers to being delivered out of the hand of Pharaoh and his hosts; consequently, the children of Israel were saved from destruction.

We certainly should get an idea from this as to what the word *salvation* actually means. Without exception, it refers to what Jesus did for us in the giving of Himself on the Cross as a sacrifice. This satisfied the demands of a thrice-holy God and, thereby, delivers the sinner from the clutches of Satan because all sin has been atoned. As sin is the legal right that Satan has to hold man in bondage, with all sin atoned, Satan has lost his authority. So, an authority he presently exerts is a pseudo-authority. In other words, any sinner can turn to Christ if he so desires, and every bondage of sin will then be broken. Every Christian can look to Christ and the Cross, and whatever authority that Satan has exerted over him will quickly fade. It is all in the Word, as given by Paul: Jesus Christ and Him crucified (I Cor. 1:23).

HABITATION

"I will prepare Him an habitation," probably means in the Hebrew, *"I will glorify Him."* This is agreed upon by most of the Hebrew scholars.

Moses was remonstrating by using the phrase, *"my father's God,"* that the Lord had given promises to Abraham, Isaac, and Jacob. Those promises had been kept in totality.

Not one had fallen to the ground. As a result, Moses said, "I will exalt Him."

The pronouns He, Him, Thy, Thou, and Thee, as they refer to the Lord, are found 33 times in this psalm! How significant and how searching is this! How entirely different from most modern hymnology! So many hymns today (if they deserve to be called hymns) are full of maudlin sentimentality instead of divine adoration. They announce our love to God instead of His love for us. They recount our experiences instead of His mercies. They tell more of human attainments instead of Christ's atonement. As stated, it's a sad index of our low state of spirituality! Different far was this song of Moses and Israel: *"I will exalt Him,"* sums it all up.

REDEMPTION

The first song of Scripture has been rightly designated the song of redemption, for it proceeded from the hearts of a redeemed people. From all of this, we find there are two parts to redemption. They are:

1. Redemption is by *purchase,* which speaks of what Christ did at the Cross.
2. Redemption is by *power,* which speaks of the power of the Holy Spirit that is made possible by the Cross of Christ.

Some believers get *redemption* and *ransom* confused. Ransoming is but a part of redemption. The two are clearly distinguished in Scripture.

It is said of Christ in Hosea 13:14: *"I will 'ransom' them from the power of the grave; I will 'redeem' them from death."* Again we read: *"For the* LORD *has 'redeemed' Jacob, and 'ransomed' him from the hand of him who was stronger than he"* (Jer. 31:11).

Ransom is the payment of the price, which Jesus did at the cross. Redemption, of which ransom is but a part, in the full sense, is the deliverance of the persons for whom the price was paid. It is the latter that is obviously the all-important item. Of what use is the ransom if the captive be not released? Without actual emancipation, there will be no song of praise. Who would ever thank a ransomer who left him in bondage?

DELIVERANCE

The Greek word for *redemption* is rendered *"deliverance"* in Hebrews 11:35.

In the book of Revelation, Jesus is pictured both as a *"Lamb,"* which refers to the purchaser, and as a *"Lion,"* which refers to the powerful emancipator.

On the Passover night, Israel was secured from the *doom* of the Egyptians. At the Red Sea, they were delivered from the *power* of the Egyptians. Thus delivered (*redeemed*), they sang. It is only a ransomed and redeemed people, conscious of their deliverance, who can really praise the Lord the deliverer.

Not only is worship impossible for those yet dead in trespasses and sins, but also intelligent worship cannot be rendered by professing Christians who are in doubt as to their standing before God, and necessarily so. Praise and joy are essential elements of worship, but how can those who question their experience in the Beloved, who are not certain whether they would go to heaven or hell should they die this moment, be joyful and thankful? It's impossible!

Uncertainty and doubt beget fear and distrust and not gladness and adoration.

A MAN OF WAR

"The LORD *is a man of war: the* LORD *is His name"* (Ex. 15:3).

The Lord is a man of war in every capacity. He had just defeated the mightiest field army on the face of the earth, and did so without using a single human soldier. But to be frank, His capacity in the realm of spiritual warfare is of even greater magnitude.

At the Cross of Calvary, the Lord Jesus totally and completely defeated Satan. He did it not through mortal combat, as would be obvious, but rather by taking away Satan's authority. Sin gives Satan the authority to do what he does, but with all sin atoned, as it was at the Cross, his authority has been removed. If it seems as if he presently has authority, we must remember also, as stated, that it is a pseudo-authority. This refers to an authority which Christians allow Satan to have simply because they do not know their place and position in Christ. The reason they don't know that place and position is simply because they do not understand the Cross. While most Christians do understand the Cross as it refers to salvation, they have little knowledge at all as it refers to sanctification. This is the tragedy!

The Lord is the man of war, not we ourselves. When we try to place ourselves in that position, we get defeated every time. In fact, the only fight that we are called upon to fight is *"the good fight of faith"* (I Tim. 6:12).

"The LORD *is His name,"* could be translated, *"Jehovah, the alone-existing One."* Before Him, all other existence fades and falls into nothingness.

Let us say it again: In looking through the various notes of this song, we do not find a single note about *"self,"* its doings, its sayings, its feelings, or its fruits. It is all about Jehovah from beginning to end, and that's the way it ought to be.

PHARAOH

"Pharaoh's chariots and his host has He cast into the sea: his chosen captains also are drowned in the Red Sea" (Ex. 15:4).

It is not known as to exactly what percentage of Pharaoh's army is included here. Irrespective, the ones who did come after Israel seemingly were the chosen and the best. For sure, his finest charioteers were lost, as well as his *"chosen captains."*

Another thing is for sure: it would be some time before Egypt's army was back up to full potential.

THEY SANK

"The depths have covered them: they sank into the bottom as a stone" (Ex. 15:5).

The warriors who fought in chariots commonly wore coats of mail, composed of bronze plates sewn onto a linen base and overlapping one another. These coats covered the arms to the elbow and descended nearly to the knee. Consequently, being as heavy as they were, these warriors would have sunk at once, even without a struggle, like a stone or a lump of lead, as the waters cascaded down upon them.

THE RIGHT HAND OF THE LORD

"Your right hand, O LORD, is become glorious in power: Your right hand, O LORD, has dashed in pieces the enemy" (Ex. 15:6).

The *"right hand,"* as it refers to the Lord, is used as a figure of speech. It signifies power. Consequently, when it is said that Christ is now seated *"on the right hand of the Majesty on high,"* though that is literally true, it also signifies power.

That right hand of power, as it refers to the Lord, can and will be used on our behalf, as well, providing our faith is placed 100 percent in Christ and what Christ has done for us at the Cross. Then the Holy Spirit, who is God, and who can do all things, will saturate the believer with power.

What kind of power?

This is not power or authority over other people, but rather over the spirits of darkness (Lk. 10:19; Eph. 6:11-18).

While, of course, all Christians fight the Devil, we must understand that it's always indirectly. Christ has already defeated him, and we fight him simply by fighting the good fight of faith, which refers to faith in Christ and His Cross.

THE WRATH OF GOD

"And in the greatness of Your excellency You have over-thrown them who rose up against You: You sent forth Your wrath, which consumed them as stubble" (Ex. 15:7).

The verbs in this verse are future. Consequently, it should read, *"You will overthrow them who rise up against You."* Then, *"You will send forth Your wrath."*

The last phrase, *"Which consumed them as stubble,"* is present tense and concerns the victory over the Egyptians.

So, in this verse, we have an account not only of what the Lord has done regarding the Egyptians, but the promise that He will fight thusly for us as well!

The first song in the Bible was sung on a shore heaped with dead men — an appalling scene of divine wrath — and the last song in the Bible will be sung in a scene of greater wrath and destruction (Rev., Chpt. 19). These inspired records of God's ways on earth and of His actions toward sin anger the self-righteous heart but thrill the soul of the one dependent on the righteousness of Christ.

GOD'S USE OF THE ELEMENTS

"And with the blast of Your nostrils the waters were gathered together, the floods stood upright as an heap, and the depths were congealed in the heart of the sea" (Ex. 15:8).

Moses described the east wind, which God set in motion, as *"the blast"* or *"breath of His nostrils."* He then represented the waters as *"standing in a heap"* on either side and the depths as *"congealed."*

Concerning the word *congealed,* some have taken this phrase to mean that the waters froze; however, considering the climate of Egypt, that is unlikely, although it definitely could have happened.

Still others have asked the question, "Are we justified in taking literally the strong expressions of a highly wrought poetic description?"

We definitely are justified. It is the Holy Spirit Who gave Moses these very words, and to be sure, as highly poetic as they might be, still, the description in no way stretches the truth as it regards what God has done, and above all, what He can do. In fact, with Him, all things are possible!

THE ENEMY SAID

"The enemy said, I will pursue, I will overtake, I will divide the spoil; my lust shall be satisfied upon them; I will draw my sword, my hand shall destroy them" (Ex. 15:9).

This verse is very important simply because it shows the thoughts of the soldiers who flocked to Pharaoh's standard, in regard to the pursuit of the children of Israel.

The words, *"I will divide the spoil,"* proclaim the fact that Israel had gone out of Egypt laden with ornaments of silver and gold and, as well, accompanied by flocks and herds of great value. Pharaoh probably told these soldiers that this plunder would be theirs, and they intended to appropriate it. They then boasted, *"My hand shall destroy them."*

As well, we must not forget that the Egyptians had given the children of Israel the finest clothing that was available at that time, meaning that when they crossed the Red Sea, they did so dressed in the finest that the world had to offer of that particular day. In other words, they did not leave Egypt as beggars dressed in rags, as slaves generally wore, but dressed in the finest and loaded down with silver and gold.

What a mighty God we serve!

THE ENEMY

There is much to be learned from this statement, *"My hand shall destroy them."*

The enemy declared fully as to what they intended to do and full well meant every word; however, they were not able to do anything and, in fact, even as the next verse proclaims, were destroyed themselves.

Here's the point I wish to make: Countless times, the Devil has told you that he is going to destroy you, your children are going to be eternally lost, you're going to die from some terrible disease, you will go bankrupt, etc. But have you ever stopped to think that none of that has ever come to pass?

To be sure, if Satan could do all these things, or any part of these things, he would have done them a long time ago. He hasn't done them simply because he can't do them. He doesn't have the power! The truth is: *"You are of God, little children, and have overcome them: because greater is He* (the Holy Spirit) *who is in you, than he* (Satan) *who is in the world"* (I Jn. 4:4).

CAMPMEETING

I was preaching a particular service in one of our Campmeetings when I began to bring out this thought about Satan not being able to do what he claims that he is going to do. The power of God swept the congregation as every single Christian in the place understood what was being said. Even though my message was not yet concluded, they could not contain themselves and, therefore, began to praise God, with the entire service erupting in praise.

I want you the reader to understand fully what is being said. The enemy has said much to you. He hopes to strike fear into your heart; however, never forget, if he could do all the things that he claims he's going to do, he would have done them a long time ago. He hasn't done them because he can't do them because the power that's in you is greater than that which is in him.

So, the next time he tries to feed you his negative line, just shout the praises of God because whatever he says, you know better.

THE LORD'S ANSWER

"You did blow with Your wind, the sea covered them: they sank as lead in the mighty waters" (Ex. 15:10).

Here we have another fact that is not mentioned in the account, but yet, which is implied. The immediate cause of the return of the waters was a wind. As a strong east wind had caused the waters to part, now this new wind — that which had been devised by the Lord — must have arisen contrary to the former one, blowing from the northwest or the north. This would have driven the water of the bitter lakes southward and thus produce the effect spoken of.

WHO IS LIKE UNTO YOU?

"Who is like unto You, O LORD, among the gods? Who is like You, glorious in holiness, fearful in praises, doing wonders?" (Ex. 15:11).

The gods mentioned in this verse pertain to the gods worshipped by the Egyptians. They were pitiful up beside Jehovah. In fact, they were no gods at all, but rather figments of the imagination of evil men. If there was any power there at all, and to be sure, there was some power, it would have been in the realm of demon spirits.

In this setting, all the gods of Egypt — and the Egyptians worshipped many gods — we find the whole series of miraculous visitations, which proclaim the fact that the true God, Jehovah, should be exalted far above all the gods of the heathen.

THE THREE ATTRIBUTES OF GOD

Moses made all of this the foundation of his praise. He pointed to the three attributes of God, which cannot be equaled elsewhere. They are:

1. Holiness: in fact, God is thrice-holy, hence, the cherubim saying, *"Holy, Holy, Holy, Lord God Almighty, which was, and is, and is to come"* (Rev. 4:8).
2. Fearful: The word in the Hebrew is *yare* and means *"to revere, dreadful, reverence, terrible."* The Lord is *"fearful"* because of His holiness. He deserves praise, in fact, all the praise that humanity can give Him, because He is our Creator and, as well, has delivered us from the powers of darkness.
3. Miraculous power: He is to be viewed with awe even when we praise Him.

How entirely different is the Lord — omnipotent, immutable, sovereign, triumphant — from the feeble, changeable, disappointed, and defeated *"god"* that is the object of *"worship"* in thousands of churches! How few today glory in God's holiness! How few praise Him for His fearfulness! How few are acquainted with His wonders!

THE LORD'S RIGHT HAND

"You stretched out Your right hand, the earth swallowed them" (Ex. 15:12).

The idea is, all the Lord had to do to defeat the Egyptians — even though this was one of the mightiest armies in the world — was to simply stretch out His right hand. This means to exert His power, which was done at His Word. As a result, the *"earth swallowed them,"* which refers to the sea and, of course, is a part of the earth.

THE STRENGTH OF THE LORD

"You in Your mercy have led forth the people which You have redeemed: You have guided them in Your strength unto Your holy habitation" (Ex. 15:13).

Several things are said in this verse:

Six times the pronoun *Thou* or *Thy* is used, which we have translated into the words *"You"* or *"Your,"* signifying that salvation, and everything that pertains to that word, is found totally in God and not at all in man. As the Holy Spirit gave this song to Moses, and the Holy Spirit was most definitely the author, He emphasized the fact that the Lord had done all of this. This means that man could not receive any credit simply because man was not due any credit.

This of which I speak is probably the greatest bone of contention between God and man that one could name. God gives His way, and man attempts to change it to something else. God has one way for the sinner to be saved, and that is by simple faith and trust in Christ and what Christ has done for us at the Cross (Jn. 3:16). He also has one way of sanctification, and that is by simple faith and trust in Christ and what Christ has done for us at the Cross (Rom. 6:3-14; 8:1-11; I Cor. 1:17-18, 21, 23; 2:2, 5; Eph. 2:13-18; Col. 2:10-15).

Regrettably, most in the world try to change God's way of salvation, and sadder still, most Christians attempt to change His way of sanctification. Both parties, the unredeemed and the redeemed, revert to *"works."* It is ironic that the redeemed will shake their heads sadly at the world and plainly tell them that they cannot earn their salvation, which is certainly correct, but then they turn right around and try to earn their sanctification by the same method they have told the world it cannot be done.

REDEEMED

The word *redeemed* in Hebrew is *gaal* and means *"to deliver, to purchase, to ransom."* It also means to *"set free,"* which is the same meaning as its Greek derivative, *"to purchase the slave out of the marketplace."* God's redeemed are a people whom He has purchased for Himself to be with Him forever — *"that where I am, there you may be also."* We are redeemed to be placed in His *"holy habitation,"* which we will address momentarily.

STRENGTH

The unredeemed never think of themselves as being slaves, much less slaves to Satan, but that's exactly what they are. As such, only the strength of the Lord can extricate them from this terrible bondage of darkness. Man is only fooling himself if he thinks otherwise.

Most, if not all, believers would agree with what I've just stated, but then, some seem to think that because they are saved, thereby, new creations in Christ Jesus (II Cor. 5:17), they have the strength to sanctify themselves, i.e., to live a godly life. While they claim to trust God, to stand upon the Word, or to trust Christ, most Christians are trying to do this outside of the Cross. In other words, they do not understand the part the Cross of Christ plays in their sanctification experience, which has to do with their everyday life and living before God, which is of supreme significance.

PERSONAL STRENGTH?

The truth is, the Christian has no more personal strength after salvation than he did before salvation. While it is certainly true that we have strength, even great strength, it is all in the Holy Spirit and not at all in us. The Holy Spirit, who lives and resides within our hearts and lives (I Cor. 3:16), works and functions in one way, and one way only. That one way is the Cross of Christ. Everything the Holy Spirit does is within the parameters of the finished work of Christ, which has given Him the legal right to do what He does (Rom. 8:1-2, 11). In other words, it was the Cross that opened up the way simply because the sin debt was totally and completely paid, making it possible for the Holy Spirit to live within our hearts and lives on a permanent basis. This means that we the believers must anchor our faith at all times in the great sacrifice of Christ. Listen again to Paul: *"But God forbid that I should glory* (boast), *save in the Cross of our Lord Jesus Christ, by whom the world is crucified unto me, and I unto the world"* (Gal. 6:14).

To be frank, our salvation and our victory depend upon three things:

1. The Cross.
2. Our faith in Christ and the Cross.
3. That which gives the Holy Spirit latitude to work (the Cross).

HOLY HABITATION

It is clear here that through divine revelation, Moses knew there would be a place in the land of Canaan where God would *"put His name"* (Deut. 12:5, 11, 14; 14:23-24; 16:6, 11; 26:2). It seems also that he knew where that place would be — Jerusalem.

√But, as most, if not all, the Old Testament prophecies, it has even a greater reference than the temple in Jerusalem. In fact, in its conclusion, it is referring to the Holy Spirit ultimately dwelling within the child of God.

Jesus told His disciples, *"And I will pray the Father, and He shall give you another Comforter* (Helper), *that He may abide with you forever; even the Spirit of truth; whom the world cannot receive, because it sees Him not, neither knows Him: but you know Him; for He dwells with you, and shall be in you"* (Jn. 14:16-17).

Then Paul said, *"Do you not know that you are the temple of God, and that the Spirit of God dwells with you, and shall be in you"* (I Cor. 3:16; Jn. 14:17).

To verify, the great apostle repeated himself by saying: *"Do you not know that you are the temple of God, and that the Spirit of God dwells in you?"* (I Cor. 3:16).

THE DWELLING PLACE OF GOD

First of all, one might say, *"God dwelt in the sacrifices, which began at the very dawn of time"* (Gen., Chpt. 4). In this manner, sins could be forgiven and the Lord could have communion with the sinner, but only in a limited way. The reason was that the blood of bulls and goats could not take away sins (Heb. 10:4). So, this meant that the terrible sin debt remained.

Then, whenever the plans for the tabernacle were given, God dwelt between the mercy seat and the cherubim in the tabernacle. He then dwelt in the temple in the same manner, but His ultimate dwelling place, which was brought about by what Jesus did at the Cross, was and is the human heart. Before the Cross, He could not make the human heart and life His habitation simply because, as stated, the blood of bulls and goats was woefully insufficient to take away sins (Heb. 10:4). But when Jesus came and died on the Cross, He took away all sin, at least for all who will believe (Jn. 1:29).

By simple faith in Christ, one becomes *"His holy habitation."* This is a new standing, which means that we are literally placed in Christ, which is made possible by the Cross and our faith in that finished work. In fact, this is the position of all believers in the Lord Jesus Christ. *"For Christ also has once suffered for sins* (the Cross)*, the just for the unjust, that He might bring us to God"* (I Pet. 3:18). This is our place as His redeemed.

GOD'S WHOLE MORAL NATURE

With God's whole moral nature having been satisfied in the death of Christ, He can now rest in us in perfect complacency. Jesus said, *"At that day* (after Christ had gone to the Cross) *you shall know that I am in My Father, and you in Me, and I in you"* (Jn. 14:20).

The old hymn says,

So near, so very near to God,
I nearer cannot be,
For in the person of His Son,
I am as near as He.

This place was all made possible by the Cross and our faith in that great sacrifice. It is indeed accorded to us in grace, but nonetheless, in righteousness, so that not only are all the attributes of God's character concerned in bringing us there, but He Himself is also glorified by it. It is an immense thought, and one which, when held in power, imparts both strength and energy to our souls—that we are even now brought to God.

The whole distance — measured by the death of Christ on the Cross when He was made sin for us (a sin offering), which means that He took upon Himself the total and complete sin penalty—has been bridged over, and our position of nearness is marked by the place He now occupies as glorified by the right hand of God (Heb. 1:3).

In fact, even when we are transported to heaven itself, we shall not be nearer, as it regards our *position,* than we are now because it is *"in Christ."*

IN CHRIST

Because we are *"in Christ"* and have that *standing* as the result of the Cross, God looks for a *state* corresponding with our *standing.*

Pink says, "State and walk must ever flow from a known relationship. Unless therefore we are taught the truth of our standing before God, we shall never answer to it in our souls, or in our walk before God."

This is the great truth, the manner of sanctification for the saint, that I am continually trying to bring out in this volume. I am doing so, addressing it from every angle that I know, even in the fear of being overly repetitious. But I do so because I realize how hard Satan fights this truth of truths, and due to the flesh, how difficult it is for the believer to grasp what is being said.

The Lord has given me the revelation of how to live for God, which is not new but actually that which He gave to Paul, and if I said otherwise, I would not be telling the truth. But yet, it is so difficult to get Christians out of the spiritual lethargy in which they sleep. That's why Paul said, *"Therefore let us not sleep, as do others; but let us watch and be sober"* (I Thess. 5:6).

THE VICTORY OF THE SAINTS

"The people shall hear, and be afraid: sorrow shall take hold on the inhabitants of Palestina.

"Then the dukes of Edom shall be amazed; the mighty men of Moab, trembling shall take hold upon them; all the inhabitants of Canaan shall melt away.

"Fear and dread shall fall upon them; by the greatness of Your arm they shall be as still as a stone; till Your people pass over, O LORD, till the people pass over, which You have purchased" (Ex. 15:14-16).

How so very much this portrays the fact that the doubt and unbelief of 10 of the 12 spies sent into Canaan was so unnecessary (Num., Chpt. 13). It brought untold sorrow and heartache, even the death of that generation in the wilderness.

And why not! The inhabitants of Canaan had all heard of the great miracles performed by the Lord in Egypt, and especially the miracle of the Red Sea.

This is evidenced by what Rahab said:

"I know that the LORD *has given you the land, and that your terror is fallen upon us, and that all the inhabitants of the land faint because of you.*

"For we have heard how the LORD *dried up the water of the Red Sea for you, when you came out of Egypt; and what you did unto the two kings of the Amorites, who were on the other side Jordan, Sihon and Og, whom you utterly destroyed.*

"And as soon as we had heard these things, our hearts did melt, neither did there remain any more courage in any man, because of you: for the LORD *your God, He is God in Heaven above, and in earth beneath"* (Josh. 2:9-11).

WHAT JESUS HAS DONE

All of this portrays in type what Christ accomplished at the Cross when He *"spoiled principalities and powers* (fallen angels and demon spirits), *where He made a show of them openly, triumphing over them in it"* (Col. 2:14-15). Just as these enemy nations feared Israel, likewise, all fallen angels and demon spirits, even Satan himself, fear the child of God who understands and knows that he has *"passed over"* into our inheritance, which was purchased for us by the Lord Jesus Christ. In fact, the Scripture portrays Satan as a coward.

James said, "*Submit yourselves therefore to God. Resist the Devil, and he will flee from you*" (James 4:7).

HOW DO WE RESIST THE DEVIL?

We resist him successfully in one way, and one way only, and that one way is the way of faith (Heb., Chpt. 11). This means that we aren't to try to use our own strength and ability, whatever that is, but rather faith.

What do we mean, resist him by faith?

Whenever faith is addressed in the Bible, either directly or indirectly, it speaks of Christ and what Christ did at the Cross. In other words, the Cross of Christ is to ever be the object of our faith.

Satan will do everything in his power to move our faith from the Cross to other things. To be sure, he doesn't care too very much what those other things are, or even how holy they might be in their own right. Most of the time, he will use preachers preaching false messages in order to carry out this task. Tragically and sadly, most of the preaching done presently, as it regards living for God, is leading people's faith away from the Cross instead of to the Cross. This is the sure road of disaster.

While it is certainly true that most of this preaching of which I speak is done through ignorance, still, much of it is also in the realm of unbelief.

ENEMIES OF THE CROSS

For instance, the doctrine of the Word of Faith preachers is a doctrine that is totally opposed to the Cross. In fact, they are *"enemies of the Cross,"* even as Paul described (Phil. 3:18-19).

Even in the denominations that claim to believe in the Cross, they little preach the Cross, if at all, but rather preach humanistic psychology.

So, the believer resists the Devil by making certain that his faith is anchored in the Cross of Christ, and that it remains in the Cross. This is the *"good fight of faith"* that he is called upon to fight constantly (I Tim. 6:12).

Now, what I've given you is a tremendous truth. It really doesn't matter which way Satan comes against you, whether it's in the realm of temptation to commit immorality, to succumb to depression, or any one of a thousand other things which we could name. Your defense is Christ, and more particularly, what He did for you in His finished work. That's why Paul said to the Corinthians: *"I determined not to know anything among you, save Jesus Christ, and Him crucified"* (I Cor. 2:2).

I remind our Word of Faith friends that the Holy Spirit through Paul didn't say: "For I determined not to know anything among you, save Jesus Christ, and Him *resurrected,"* which is what some others teach, but rather *"Him crucified."*

Oh yes, Paul most definitely preached the resurrection, but his main theme was always the Cross of Christ.

THE INHERITANCE

"You shall bring them in, and plant them in the mountain of Your inheritance, in the place, O LORD, *which You have made for You to dwell in, in the sanctuary, O* LORD, *which Your hands have established"* (Ex. 15:17).

This great song proclaims who God is, what He did, and how He did it.

It also proclaims, as given in Verse 17, that all of this was done for a purpose. It was to bring the children of Israel to the place of the *"Lord's inheritance,"* which He had made for them to *"dwell in."* As stated, for the children of Israel, it referred to Canaanland; however, its total meaning has to do with the believer's position in Christ, for biblical history has always strained toward this conclusion.

The phrase, *"Which Your hands have established,"* speaks of something already done, in other words, past tense.

This means that even before the children of Israel reached Canaanland, God had already ordained that the land would be theirs, despite the enemies which inhabited it. Likewise, He has established the fact that we as believers should be totally and completely victorious, all in Christ, which means that sin shall not have dominion over us (Rom. 6:14).

PARTAKERS OF CHRIST

Now, regrettably, many Israelites died lost — even before getting to the land and even after being in the land — because of a lack of faith. It is the same with the modern believer.

Despite the fact that God has already ordained our victory, if we as believers harden our hearts against the way of the Lord, which is Christ and Him crucified, we too can lose our way (Heb. 6:4-6; 10:26-29).

The apostle said: *"For we are made partakers of Christ, if we hold the beginning of our confidence* (continue to exhibit faith in Christ and the Cross) *steadfast unto the end;*

"While it is said, Today if you will hear His voice, harden not your hearts, as in the provocation (as did Israel).

"For some, when they had heard, did provoke: howbeit not all who came out of Egypt by Moses (it seems that some repented and continued to believe).

"But with whom was He grieved forty years? was it not with them who had sinned (who lost faith)*, whose carcasses fell in the wilderness?*

"And to whom swore He that they should not enter into His rest, but to them who believed not?

"So we see that they could not enter in because of unbelief (failure to trust Christ and His finished work)*"* (Heb. 3:14-19).

SIN AND THE BELIEVER

God will never overthrow the believer because of sin, even as vile as that sin might be, if the believer faithfully repents and continues to trust Christ, at least as best as he knows how. But, of course, the bondage of sin is present in a believer's life simply because he does not understand his place and position in Christ, which was and is afforded by the Cross. Not understanding that it is the Cross that has guaranteed us all things, and that we must, thereby, keep our faith in the Cross of Christ, sadly and regrettably, most Christians place their faith in other things. This is a guarantee that sin will, in some way, dominate their hearts and lives.

As stated, God will not overthrow the believer for sins within his heart and life, with the exception of the one sin of unbelief. That speaks of the believer losing faith in Christ and what Christ has done at the Cross, rather advocating other things. Because the Cross is the great foundational truth of the atonement, for this sin of unbelief, an individual who was once saved can, thereby, take himself out of the salvation of the Lord and be lost. Faith is what gets us in, and faith in Christ and His Cross is what keeps us in. If we lose such faith, we have lost salvation (Heb. 6:4-6; 10:26-29).

SPIRITUAL ADULTERY

If the Lord threw believers over because of sins of the flesh, etc., to be quite frank, there wouldn't be any believers left; however, let it be ever understood that any type of sin registered in the heart and life of the believer is an occasion for misery. This is not the normal Christian experience. In fact, such a position pictures the believer as living in a state of spiritual adultery (Rom. 7:1-4). This simply means that the believer is married to Christ but is being unfaithful to Christ by placing his or her faith in things other than Christ and what Christ has done for us at the Cross. As stated, Paul classified such action as *"spiritual adultery."* There is no joy or peace of mind in such a life, even though the believer is saved. Joy and peace can be found only in total and complete victory, which is what God intends for us to have, and which we most certainly can have if we will simply follow God's prescribed order of victory.

OUR GOD REIGNS

"The LORD shall reign forever and ever" (Ex. 15:18).

This word closes this great and beautiful song. The song ends as it began — with *"The Lord."* Faith views the eternal future without a tremor.

Let us never forget that we are able by faith to enter this eternal future all because of the following:

"Having therefore, brethren, boldness to enter into the Holiest by the blood of Jesus ... Let us draw near with a true heart in full assurance of faith ... Let us hold fast the profession of our faith without wavering" (Heb. 10:19-23).

Once again, let the believer understand that it is all by faith, and more particularly, it speaks of faith in Christ, and more particularly still, faith in what He did for us in the shedding of His precious blood, which He did at the Cross, and which paid the price for our redemption.

Once again, I remind our Word of Faith friends that we *"enter into the Holiest,"* not by the resurrection of Jesus, but rather the blood of Jesus, which speaks of Him shedding such at the Cross.

VICTORY

"For the horse of Pharaoh went in with his chariots and with his horsemen into the sea, and the LORD brought again the waters of the sea upon them; but the children of Israel went on dry land in the midst of the sea" (Ex. 15:19).

It seems that Miriam, Moses' sister, led Israel in worship. When it says, *"And Miriam answered them,"* it is speaking of the men singing and the women answering them under the leadership of Miriam.

The timbrels, as mentioned in Verse 20, suggest the pleasure of the Holy Spirit in using such to accompany the singing, which speaks of musical instruments.

There was great rejoicing as it regarded the great miracle performed by the Lord in opening the Red Sea and, as well, drowning the Egyptian army. Giving vent to this great happiness and joy, the women of Israel, who could have numbered a half million or more, began to lead Israel in *"dancing before the Lord,"* with worship and praise.

We are commanded here to *"sing you to the LORD, for He has triumphed gloriously."* This refers not only to Israel of old, but to all modern believers, as well, and, in fact, every believer who has ever lived.

JESUS CHRIST AND HIM CRUCIFIED

A part of the song sung by Miriam and the women of Israel is given in this verse. In other words, it is a compendium of what they sang.

We as believers are to ever tell what the Lord has done for us, and most important of all, we are to proclaim the salvation that He has given us, how He saved us, and by what means, which is Jesus Christ and Him crucified (I Cor. 1:23).

In fact, after the time of the great tribulation foretold by Jesus (Mat. 24:21), those who come out of the great tribulation, both Jews and Gentiles, having gained victory over the beast, will sing this song again in Heaven. It is called *"the song of Moses the servant of God, and the song of the Lamb"* (Rev. 15:1-4).

MIRIAM THE PROPHETESS

"And Miriam the prophetess, the sister of Aaron, took a timbrel in her hand; and all the women went out after her with timbrels and with dances" (Ex. 15:20).

Miriam was the sister of both Moses and Aaron. She is the first woman whom the Bible honors with the title of *prophetess*.

Pulpit says of her: "Miriam is regarded by the Prophet Micah (Mic. 6:4), as having had a share in the deliverance of Israel, and claims the prophetic gift in Numbers 12:2. Her claim appears to be allowed both in the present passage, and in Numbers 12:6-8, where the degree of her inspiration, however, is placed below that of Moses."

We find throughout Israel and, as well, in the New Testament that women often played a major role in the work of God. As they were participants of the *"callings,"* as is here made evident, Deborah was also selected by the Lord to be the judge of Israel during the particular time of the judges.

She was the fourth person to occupy that position. Along with her military commander, Barak, she won a great victory over the Canaanites (Judg. 4:1-5:31).

On the inaugural day of the church, so to speak, Peter quoted the Prophet Joel: *"And it shall come to pass in the last days, says God, I will pour out of My Spirit upon all flesh: and your sons and your daughters shall prophesy."*

To emphasize the point, the Holy Spirit had him say it again: *"And on My servants and on My handmaidens I will pour out in those days of My Spirit; and they shall prophesy"* (Acts 2:17-18).

TO PROPHESY

The Greek word for *prophesy* is *propheteuo* and means *"to foretell events, or to speak under inspiration."*

So, this tells us that women are called to preach the same as men.

Paul said, *"But I suffer not a woman to teach, nor to usurp authority over the man, but to be in silence"* (I Tim. 2:12).

First of all, the order that God has set up is that man is in authority. The apostle also said, *"For Adam was first formed, then Eve"* (I Tim. 2:13).

The word *authority* proclaims the rule that if a man is available who has the calling of pastor, he should pastor the church, and not a woman, even though she might have the calling, as well, of pastor (Eph. 4:11). If no man is available, she could feel free to serve in that capacity.

Silence in the Greek is *hesuchia* and means *"distance from bustle or language, quietness, silence."* The word goes back to *authority*, referring to the fact that while a woman is certainly allowed, and even encouraged, to speak her mind, and that her wisdom is equal to that of the man, still, she is not to push forward, but rather to remember her place. If everything is done in God's order, the ability of any and every individual is given opportunity.

Other than the order which the Holy Spirit has set up, and which is obvious, Paul said, *"For you are all the children of God by faith in Christ Jesus. There is neither male nor female: for you are all one in Christ Jesus"* (Gal. 3:26, 28).

GREAT REJOICING

The inspired scene that unfolds before us is a wonder to behold, to say the very least. There could have been as many as 500,000, or even more, women playing tambourines and dancing before the Lord. As we've stated, the first reaction to the mighty deliverance was great rejoicing, as will always be the case in one way or the other, when a person comes to Christ and is, therefore, delivered from the clutches of the Evil One. Concerning the women, sin had come into the human race through the woman, but now her heart was lifted up in praise, which testified in itself of victory over it.

It seems that this great celebration was part rehearsed and part spontaneous.

We have some reason to believe that Moses may have also been an accomplished singer. He not only sang this song, but, as well, the Lord gave him Psalm 90, and more than likely, even Psalm 91, both of which are songs. Most of the time when people write songs, they also have the ability to sing those songs.

The Scripture says that Moses and the children of Israel sang this song, as given to us in Chapter 15. Consequently, it would seem that the Lord first gave the song to Moses, with him having any number of scribes to hurriedly make copies, which could have numbered into many hundreds.

He could have pulled together any number of people, both men and women — for the Scripture says *"the children of Israel,"* which included both — and then taught them this song. Quite possibly, as the Holy Spirit inspired Moses to write this song, He could very well have inspired the people to learn the song quickly and to sing it, which is, no doubt, what happened.

DEMONSTRATIVE

At any rate, many thousands began to sing because of the great joy that filled their hearts. It seems that Miriam spontaneously took a timbrel in her hand, and playing the instrument, which refers to keeping rhythm, she began to dance before the Lord, with many thousands of women then joining her. As stated, that must have been quite a sight.

I cannot recall any Campmeeting we've ever had where the people were that demonstrative, but we certainly ought to be!

Let it be understood, as well, that the dancing here was definitely not orchestrated or choreographed, at least as we think of such presently. As stated, it was spontaneous. In fact, this method of dancing became quite common in Jewish history. It consisted of the women, usually playing the tambourines as Miriam did here, whirling about in joy before the Lord. The modern method of some churches of hiring choreographers can be constituted as nothing but the flesh. When the joy of the Lord fills the heart to such an extent that the women cannot keep still but must dance before the Lord, which will always be in a fashion that glorifies God and not the flesh, this should ever be desired. We have two problems in the modern church:

1. The first problem is spiritual deadness. In other words, there is absolutely no emotion whatsoever. Such an attitude and direction are not at all scriptural, as should be obvious.

2. The second problem is that there are all types of emotions, but generated by the flesh. Both are equally bad. If the Spirit of God has His way, there definitely will be emotion, but it will be the joy of the Lord and not an operation of the flesh. In fact, spiritual deadness and mere emotionalism are both of the flesh, although in opposite directions.

SING TO THE LORD

"And Miriam answered them, Sing you to the Lord, *for He has triumphed gloriously; the horse and his rider has He thrown into the sea"* (Ex. 15:21).

The phrase, *"And Miriam answered them,"* seems to imply that the men would sing a refrain, and then the women would answer by singing the refrain again. Whether they did this while dancing, or whether some danced and some sang, we aren't told.

At any rate, their worship and praise proclaimed the Lord as the triumphant One in every capacity.

The writer of Psalm 149 said:

"Praise you the Lord. *Sing unto the* Lord *a new song, and His praise in the congregation of saints.*

"Let Israel rejoice in Him who made him: let the children of Zion be joyful in their King.

"Let them praise His name in the dance: let them sing praises unto Him with the timbrel and harp.

"For the Lord *takes pleasure in His people: He will beautify the meek with salvation.*

"Let the saints be joyful in glory: let them sing aloud upon their beds.

"Let the high praises of God be in their mouth ..." (Ps. 149:1-6).

THE WILDERNESS

"So Moses brought Israel from the Red Sea, and they went out into the wilderness of Shur; and they went three days in the wilderness, and found no water" (Ex. 15:22).

God tests faith in order to strengthen and enrich it.

Israel journeyed three days in the wilderness and found no water. When water was found, there was an added trial—the water was bitter, which is a type of this world and what it has to offer.

Not to be thankful (Rom. 1:21) and to murmur lead to greater sins. Israel murmured, and their unbelief deepened as they murmured.

The smitten tree was cast into the waters, and the waters became sweet, which is a type of the Cross of Christ being placed into the bitterness of our souls. Thus, life may be sweetened if in the energy of faith, a crucified Saviour is introduced into it.

The healing mentioned here refers not only to the physical healing of the body but, as well, the spiritual healing of the soul.

The refreshment enjoyed at Elim suggested that which would come at the advent of Christ. The Lord sent out 12 apostles and 70 others to revive His weary inheritance with the tidings that the kingdom of Heaven was at hand.

As previously stated, we must understand that the Lord led the children of Israel into the wilderness. To be sure, this particular wilderness was about as inhospitable as anything could ever be.

A MATTER OF SOVEREIGN GRACE

Regrettably, the wilderness experience is needed by all Christians. First, the trials and testings of the wilderness make manifest the evil of our hearts and the incurable corruption of the flesh. These trials and tests are necessary in order that we may be humbled.

Second, the entrance into the inheritance itself is also solely a matter of sovereign grace, seeing that there is no worthiness and no *"good thing"* in us.

While the wilderness may, and will, make manifest the weakness of God's saints, as well as our failures, this is only to magnify the power and mercy of Him who brought us into the place of testing. Further, we must understand that God always has in view our ultimate good.

So, we find that the *"wilderness"* gives us not only a revelation of ourselves, but it also manifests the ways of God.

After the Red Sea crossing, the children of Israel went *"three days into the wilderness,"* which speaks of resurrection, for Christ was raised from the dead three days after His burial (I Cor. 15:4).

And yet, despite the resurrection type, we find that almost immediately, they met with testing — no water, at least that which was useable.

While the world may look very attractive to the unbeliever, to the man of faith, it is simply a wilderness — barren and desolate. No one thinks of making his home in such a place, and neither should the believer become too attached to this world. It is merely the place through which man journeys from time to eternity, and it is *faith* that makes the difference in the way in which men regard this world.

GOD ALONE CAN SATISFY THE HUMAN HEART

The wilderness having no water is the first lesson that our experience is designed to teach us. There is nothing down here that can in any wise minister to that life which we have received from Christ. The pleasures of sin and the attractions of the world no longer satisfy. It is quite the contrary. These things that formerly charmed us now repel us. The companionship we used to find so pleasing has become distasteful. The things which delight the ungodly only cause us to groan.

In fact, the Christian who is in communion with his Lord finds absolutely nothing around him that will or can refresh his thirsty soul. For him, the shallow cisterns of this world have run dry. His cry will be that of the psalmist: *"O God, You are my God; early will I seek You; my soul thirsts for You, my flesh longs for You in a dry and thirsty land, where no water is"* (Ps. 63:1).

God alone can satisfy the longings of the heart. That's why Jesus said, *"If any man thirst, let him come unto Me, and drink"* (Jn. 7:37). So must he continue to go to Him who alone has the Water of Life.

We are going to find that the first lesson the Lord taught the children of Israel was the lesson of the Cross, just as He taught this lesson to the first family (Gen., Chpt. 4).

BITTER WATERS

"And when they came to Marah, they could not drink of the waters of Marah, for they were bitter: therefore the name of it was called Marah" (Ex. 15:23).

The word *Marah* actually means *"bitter."* Whether Israel gave it this name, or it had already been given this name, we aren't told; however, the likelihood is that it had borne this name for some time. This is a test of faith, and as we shall see, Israel didn't meet this test too very well.

In a sense, every single thing that comes the way of the child of God is a test of sorts. Of course, some of these tests are of far greater magnitude than others; nevertheless, everything is a test, and we must look at every situation in this light.

How will we react? Will we trust God or murmur and complain?

Great blessings tell us who God is; adversity tells us what we are!

MURMURING

"And the people murmured against Moses, saying, What shall we drink?" (Ex. 15:24).

Three days before, the children of Israel were rejoicing on the shores of the Red Sea. Now, some 72 hours later, they are *"murmuring against Moses,"* which speaks of complaining, and which was to very soon cause them tremendous problems.

Murmuring and complaining present a lack of faith, but the problem was not so easily recognizable.

Probably one could say without fear of exaggeration that the children of Israel had faith, but it was in the wrong object. It seemed to have been in Moses. When everything was going well, he was their hero. At the slightest adversity, the tables turned.

As we shall see, and as the Lord would teach them, their faith had to be in the Cross of Christ. Lacking that, their problems would multiply, and fast. There is only one way to live this life, to walk in victory, to be what God wants us to be, and to have the joy of the Lord, which is the more abundant life promised by Christ. That way is to understand that everything that comes to us as believers comes totally and completely by and through the Cross of Christ. As we've already said innumerable times, and will continue to say, the believer must anchor his faith in that great sacrifice. Then the Holy Spirit will work mightily with him, and with the Holy Spirit being God, there is nothing He cannot do. The believer is then guaranteed success; otherwise, the believer is guaranteed failure (Rom. 6:3-14; 8:1-2, 11; I Cor. 1:23; 2:2; Col. 2:10-15).

THE BITTERNESS OF SOUL

The bitterness portrayed here proclaims not only the condition of this present world, but also what it produces. There are untold millions of people who have suffered bitter experiences in life. Many of these have suffered sexual or mental abuse as a child, which has left them emotionally disturbed.

As a result, there is bitterness of soul, which, without the help of the Lord, that person cannot shake off. Or, life has dealt the person a bitter blow, with the individual harboring unforgiveness, etc., which occasions bitterness.

To be frank, these are not isolated situations. The problem is actually pandemic. In much of this, many actually hold a grudge against God. They feel that He could have prevented whatever it was that happened, and in their heart of hearts, they harbor resentment against Him.

When we get to Verse 25 of Chapter 15 of Exodus, I'm going to tell you how to have total and complete victory over this terrible problem. In fact, that which we will relate to you is the only manner of victory, with there being no other. However, I want to first deal with the manner in which the world attempts to address this problem, which sounds good to the carnal ear, but which, in reality, is of no help at all.

INNER HEALING

From the world of humanistic psychology has come the phrase *"inner healing,"* which, as stated, sounds good to the carnal mind and ear. To be frank, there definitely is such a thing as inner healing, but not in the way that humanistic psychology proposes.

While all psychologists, I suppose, will use the term *inner healing*, mostly, each of them has a different interpretation as to how the problem is to be addressed — all of it wrong simply because what they are proposing is not the Word of God.

Sadly, many of those who refer to themselves as Christian psychologists actually propose for this malady that the individual in question forgive God.

HUMANISTIC PSYCHOLOGY

Whatever nuance or direction the psychologist might take, almost all of them will seek to delve into the past, as it regards the individual whom they are trying to help. As it should be understood, psychological teaching, which actually had its beginnings in Sigmund Freud, who was inspired by Satan, has no miracle drug, etc., that can be prescribed for the individual. They have only one thing, and that is talk. If talk can set the captive free, then Jesus came down to this sinful world and died in vain (Gal. 2:21).

So, they get the individual to regurgitate all of the happenings of the past, which is totally unscriptural. Concerning the past, Paul said, *"Forgetting those things which are behind, reaching forth unto those things which are before, I press toward the mark for the prize of the high calling of God in Christ Jesus"* (Phil. 3:13-14).

And then, if that direction does not seem to be fruitful, the psychologist will actually make up things and plant them in the person's mind and try to convince him that that is what happened, whatever it was. However, we should understand that *talk* has never healed anyone, as ought to be obvious.

As stated, then we have so-called Christian psychologists telling people to "forgive God." In the first place, God has never done anything untoward toward anyone, so to tell people to forgive Him only exacerbates the problem, putting the person on the road of falsehood and wrong thinking.

One Christian psychologist uses as his therapeutic tool the practice of "visualization." What is that?

VISUALIZATION

The patients (victim in these circumstances) are urged to visualize certain things. They are to lie quietly with their eyes closed and visualize themselves standing by a babbling brook in a beautiful meadow with tall, stately trees around them. The scene is beautiful and peaceful. They are then to visualize Christ walking toward them, speaking softly to them, and then putting His arms around them and, thereby, healing them of all their problems.

Once again, there is nothing of this nature in the Bible. In fact, this is bordering on witchcraft. In some circles, it's called *"white magic."*

The Scripture plainly tells us, *"For whatsoever is not of faith is sin"* (Rom. 14:23).

So, what is the answer to the terrible problem of bitterness of soul?

THE CROSS

"And he cried unto the LORD; and the LORD showed him a tree, which when he had cast into the waters, the waters

were made sweet: there He made for them a statute and an ordinance, and there He proved them" (Ex. 15:25).

For the answer to this dilemma in which Israel now found herself, i.e., "bitter waters," Moses *"cried unto the LORD."*

Let me first of all say, and do so strongly, that there is no help outside of the Lord. As well, he doesn't need the advice or the counsel of Freud, or any worldly wisdom for that matter. In fact, the Holy Spirit through James plainly said, *"This wisdom descends not from above, but is earthly, sensual, devilish."*

He then said, *"But the wisdom that is from above is first pure, then peaceable, gentle, and easy to be entreated, full of mercy and good fruits, without partiality, and without hypocrisy"* (James 3:15, 17).

Peter said, *"According as His divine power has given unto us all things that pertain unto life and godliness, through the knowledge of Him who has called us to glory and virtue: Whereby are given unto us exceeding great and precious promises: that by these you might be partakers of the divine nature, having escaped the corruption that is in the world through lust"* (II Pet. 1:3-4).

So, the Lord has the answer to whatever problems we might have, whatever dilemmas in which we find ourselves, etc.

THE LORD SHOWED HIM A TREE

One doesn't have to be a Bible scholar to figure this out. The Lord was showing Moses that the answer to his dilemma was the tree. In fact, the Lord was using the tree as a type of the Cross.

I remember years ago mentioning this subject, and some brother after service tried to tell me how that the chemistry was changed in the water by this particular tree, etc.

The truth is, the Lord, by His miracle-working power, turned the bitter waters sweet. The tree, as far as its chemistry was concerned, had nothing to do with it. The Lord was using that to show Moses that the answer was found in the Cross.

Now, listen to this: The Lord had showed Israel that the *"Passover"* delivered them out of Egypt when nothing else could. It was a type of Christ and what He would do for us as our substitute on the Cross. The Red Sea crossing portrays the believer entering into the great sacrifice of Christ, as described in Romans 6:3-5. All of this constituted the salvation process, one might say.

Now that they were delivered from Egypt, no longer under the slave master's whip, and no longer slaves to that despot in any fashion, the Lord would show them that the Cross was the answer to their salvation. As well, it was the answer to their sanctification.

THE CROSS OF CHRIST

So, the first thing that the Lord portrayed to Israel through Moses was the Cross of Christ, implying strongly that this was their answer through the wilderness and into the Promised Land.

He's saying the same thing today to the modern believer. It was the Cross that got them into salvation, or rather their faith in that finished work, and it is the Cross that will effect their sanctification, in other words, how we live for the Lord on a daily basis. It is the Cross alone.

Peter said, *"The God of our fathers raised up Jesus, whom you slew and hanged on a tree"* (Acts 5:30).

Paul said, *"And when they had fulfilled all that was written of Him, they took Him down from the tree, and laid Him in a sepulcher"* (Acts 13:29).

The apostle also said, *"Christ has redeemed us from the curse of the law, being made a curse for us: for it is written, Cursed is every one who hangs on a tree"* (Gal. 3:13).

Peter also said, *"Who His own self bear our sins in His own body on the tree, that we, being dead to sins, should live unto righteousness: by whose stripes you were healed"* (I Pet. 2:24).

So, the Holy Spirit through Moses referring to the tree is picked up by both Peter and Paul, using the same terminology, which applies to the Cross.

THE TREE WAS PUT INTO THE BITTER WATERS

The believer is to appropriate the benefits of the Cross, which the Lord intends, and to do so on a continuing basis, even day-to-day. I'll tell you how to do that in a moment.

Jesus said, *"If any man will come after Me, let him deny himself* (deny his own ability, strength, etc.)*, and take up his cross daily, and follow Me"* (Lk. 9:23).

When He spoke of denying oneself, He wasn't speaking of asceticism, which is a denial of all things that are pleasurable, etc. Unfortunately, many Christians have come to the conclusion that if it's something enjoyable, then it's a sin. No, that has no bearing on what Jesus is saying here. That's what Satan would like to get people to believe, but it simply isn't true.

Living for God is the most exciting, thrilling, wonderful, and glorious life that one could ever live, and we're not under law but under grace (Rom. 6:14).

Now, notice that He said that we must take up our Cross, and even do so on a daily basis. Let's look at the first part of this statement.

TAKING UP THE CROSS

"Taking up the Cross" simply means that we understand that everything we need, in fact, everything we receive from the Lord, all and without exception, comes to us through the Cross of our Lord Jesus Christ. In other words, it's the Cross that makes it all possible, and we are speaking of what Jesus there did.

The word *daily* means that we are to appropriate these blessings afresh and anew every single morning. The Prophet Jeremiah said, *"This I recall to my mind, therefore have I hope. It is of the LORD's mercies that we are not consumed, because His compassions fail not. They are new every morning: great is Your faithfulness"* (Lam. 3:21-23).

Now, the manner in which this is done, or the how that we appropriate these benefits, is all by faith. What do we mean by that?

FAITH

None of this is a physical or material thing. It is all in the realm of the spiritual, and it is all acquired strictly by faith.

When we say *"faith,"* always and without exception, we are speaking of the believer having faith in Christ and what Christ has done at the Cross. Paul said, *"Likewise reckon you also yourselves to be dead indeed unto sin, but alive unto God through Jesus Christ our Lord"* (Rom. 6:11).

This is the believer evidencing faith in Christ and what Christ has done for us in the sacrifice of Himself.

Every believer talks about faith; however, most believers do not understand that for our faith to be recognized by God, its object must always be the finished work of Christ. Let me say that again:

It's the object of our faith that is so very important. In fact, every human being on the face of the earth has faith, but it's not faith that God will recognize. The only faith that He recognizes is faith in His Son and our Saviour, the Lord Jesus Christ, and what Christ has done, which is all proclaimed by the Word of God.

ANOTHER JESUS

Almost every Christian will talk about having faith in Christ, but let the reader understand that we must comprehend the fact that it is always Jesus Christ and Him crucified (I Cor. 1:23). In other words, if we try to divorce Christ from the Cross, we are, in effect, according to the words of Paul, preaching *"another Jesus,"* which the Lord, of course, cannot honor (II Cor. 11:4).

Millions profess to believe in Christ, and the truth is, they aren't properly aligning Christ with the Cross. No, Christ certainly is not still on the Cross, but rather seated by the right hand of the Father in heaven (Heb. 1:3). In fact, we are seated with Him in heavenly places (Eph. 2:6).

What Paul is talking about, and what Jesus was talking about as it regarded taking up the Cross daily, are the benefits of what Christ did on the Cross. I am saved because of what He did at the Cross. I am baptized with the Holy Spirit because of what He did at the Cross. I am healed because of what He did at the Cross. I am victorious because of what He did at the Cross. In fact, everything I receive from the Lord is all made possible, and without exception, through what Jesus did at the Cross. So, He must never be separated from the Cross. If, in fact, He is separated accordingly, which, regrettably, many, if not most, churches do, then pure and simple, we have accepted another Jesus, which is put forth by another spirit, which projects another gospel (II Cor. 11:4).

If it's not *"Jesus Christ and Him crucified,"* then it's not the gospel!

So, by faith, we put the Cross into the bitter waters of our lives.

THE HEALING

The Scripture then says, *"The waters were made sweet."* This means that the Lord can turn the bitterness in your heart and life into that which is sweet. In fact, He alone can do this.

As you read these words, you may think that such is beyond reach. Well, it is beyond our reach as it regards our own personal strength; however, it's definitely not beyond the reach of our Lord. In fact, this is not something that He has to do in the future. He has already healed the bitterness in your heart, and all you have to do is simply appropriate it by faith in the manner in which we have described to you.

Some may ask the question, "Will everything change immediately?"

There will definitely be a change immediately in your heart and life as you begin to realize, as the Spirit bears witness with your spirit, that you are now on the right track; however, it may take some time for the healing to be complete. Actually, the very word healing refers to a process.

However, the truth is, you are now on the right road, and while everything may not change immediately as it regards the situation, whatever it is, it will definitely ultimately change, even though it may do so little by little. Then again, regarding bitterness, the change may happen immediately with some. It has with untold thousands, and it may very well happen with you.

But that's not the point. The point is, Jesus has already healed these bitter waters, and once your faith is anchored firmly in Him and what He did at the Cross, ever making that the object of your faith, you are guaranteed victory (Rom. 8:1-2, 11).

THE STATUTE AND THE ORDINANCE

The phrase, *"There He made for them a statute and an ordinance, and there He proved them,"* refers to the promise of the next verse.

The words *proved them* refers to the testing of their faith. Regrettably, they didn't come out too well, but rather murmured and complained against Moses. However, God is merciful and gracious and didn't overthrow them, just as He is merciful and gracious to us. Thank God He is, or we wouldn't be here.

HEALING

"And said, If you will diligently hearken to the voice of the LORD *your God, and will do that which is right in His sight, and will give ear to His commandments, and keep all His statutes, I will put none of these diseases upon you, which I have brought upon the Egyptians: for I am the* LORD *who heals you"* (Ex. 15:26).

We learn several things from this verse of Scripture.

The Lord told Israel, and all of us, as well, that we must keep *"all His commandments and statutes."* He didn't say *"some,"* but rather *"all."*

Now, the truth is, no human being has ever done this, other than Christ. So, this means that in the sight of God, we are shot down, so to speak, before we even begin.

To receive the benefits of the Cross, I am obligated to do this which He commands. These are the conditions, and they will not be altered. So, what am I to do?

I am to understand that my salvation and my victory don't lie within my own perfection or the lack thereof. So, if all of this is not in me, where is it?

All that I need is in Christ. Our Lord has kept every single commandment and statute. He has done so impeccably and has done so all of the time, and He did it all for us. He is my substitute and my representative man (I Cor. 15:45-50). My trust and faith in Him grants to me all of His victory, and does so automatically and immediately.

GOD DOESN'T GIVE VICTORY TO MEN, ONLY TO CHRIST

This is where we make our mistake. We think, in essence, that He is giving victory to us. While we certainly are recipients of victory, or whatever, it is not actually to us that all of this is given. It is to Christ. God blesses Christ, and our faith in Him grants us all the blessings that He has been given. All the victory is in Christ, and my faith in Him, and my faith in Him alone, grants me His victory. In fact, this is the idea of the entire salvation process. It is all in Christ, or it is nothing at all!

Therefore, I can stand before the Lord and honestly say that through Christ and in Christ, I have kept every single commandment and statute. I sense greatly the presence of the Lord, even as I dictate these words.

Listen again to Paul: *"And you are complete in Him, which is the Head of all principality and power"* (Col. 2:10).

And then again: *"That you may stand perfect and complete in all the will of God"* (Col. 4:12).

DISEASES

The phrase, *"I will put none of these diseases upon you, which I have brought upon the Egyptians,"* proclaims the fact that the Lord is in charge of all things.

While sickness and disease originated with the fall in the garden of Eden and has come upon the human race because of sin, this is all because of a decree from the Lord.

Some Christians act as though the Lord answers to the Devil. It's the other way around. Satan answers to God! In other words, whatever it is that Satan wants to do, he can do only as the Lord gives him permission to do so. To be sure, he is not running loose, but is rather subject to the Lord at all times (Job, Chpts. 1-2).

Because of the idol worship of the Egyptians, the Lord caused certain diseases to come upon them. It is no different presently!

When men ignore God, they reap the results of their actions. While the Lord may use Satan as an instrument, which He often does, still, it is the Lord who does the directing in all things.

The Lord can withhold blessings, and He can bestow blessings. It is all predicated upon the individual and whether our faith is properly in Christ and the Cross or otherwise! Even then, our faith must be tested, and great faith must be tested greatly.

THE HEALING POWER OF GOD

The phrase, *"For I am the LORD who heals you,"* proclaims the fact that He is the healer, and He alone is the healer. The name LORD in the Hebrew, as used here, is actually *Jehovah-Ropheka*, which means *"Jehovah, the healer."* So, the Lord revealed Himself here to Moses and to the children of Israel in a more graphic way. He was telling them that He was now their healer. What a comfort that must have been!

Let the reader understand that while, in fact, they were in a wilderness, and it was unpleasant to say the least, this is where God would reveal Himself to His people even in a more advanced way. They had known Him as the deliverer; now they knew Him as the healer as well!

Let the reader also understand that as this promise was given to Moses and the children of Israel some 3,600 years ago, it is still just as appropriate now as it was then. God does not change simply because He cannot change, and we refer to His attributes. Whatever blessing He promised then, He promises now and, in fact, will ever do so.

A PERSONAL HEALING

The promise of healing is very real to me on a personal basis. If I remember correctly, the year was 1945, which means that I was 10 years old.

I had some type of physical problem, which the doctors did not seem to be able to find. My parents, in fact, took me to several doctors, but all to no avail. They ruled out malaria, plus other things, and seemed not to be able to come to a satisfactory diagnosis.

I stayed nauseated constantly and would at times go unconscious. Actually, I passed out several times at school. The last time it happened, the principal told my parents when they were called to come and get me, "Something is going to have to be done for Jimmy. And if something is not done, you're going to have to take him out of school." The principal then said, "We don't want him dying on our hands."

That's how critical that it was, and regrettably, the doctors, as stated, did not seem to be able to help.

PRAYER

I had been anointed with oil and prayed for any number of times by our pastor and others in our church but, seemingly, to no avail. However, of the following, I am very thankful.

I'm so glad that we attended a church where the pastor believed that Jesus Christ still healed the sick. Had I not been a part of such a church, I probably would not be alive today, for I believe that Satan was trying to kill me.

On the particular day in question, the day of my healing, it was a Sunday, and service had just ended. My parents were taking the pastor and his wife out to lunch. Of course, my baby sister and I were among the group.

Before going to lunch, they were to go by the home of one of the members of the church, who had been ill and had not been able to be in service that morning. They lived in a very humble dwelling, and I remember us going to the bedroom, which was at the back, and the pastor laying hands on the dear brother and praying for him.

As everyone walked back toward the front of the house, all of us stopped in the front room, in fact, bidding the lady of the house goodbye and saying something encouraging to her about her husband who was ill.

I was standing near the door, with the pastor standing behind me and my dad to his left. This scene is forever freeze-framed in my mind.

THE ANOINTING OIL

Dad said to the pastor, "Brother Culbreth, anoint Jimmy with oil and pray for him." He further added, "If the Lord doesn't do something for him, we're going to have to take him out of school."

Brother Culbreth was standing there with a little bottle of oil in his hand, with which he had just anointed the brother for whom he had come to pray. He smiled and walked toward me. He turned the bottle of oil upside-down, whereas a small amount was released onto his finger, and he anointed my head and began to pray.

Now, as stated, he had done this any number of times in the past few months. So, the question could be asked, "Why didn't the Lord heal me the other times?" I really don't have the answer to that, and I don't think anyone else does. We could probably say that He was testing our faith, and possibly that is so, but as a 10-year-old child, I didn't know that much about faith, but I did know that the Lord was the healer.

I think there are many questions that we have as it regards the Lord and the *how* of His doing of things. The Lord's ways are not our ways, but this I do know, which the Bible teaches: It teaches that Jesus Christ is still the healer (I Pet. 2:24). As well, the Lord taught us that if we don't get the answer at first, we are to keep knocking (Lk. 11:5-13).

A BALL OF FIRE

The moment the pastor anointed me with oil, he at the same time began to pray, along with all others in the room. And then it happened!

I felt something like a hot ball of fire start at the top of my head and then slowly go down through the entirety of my body, even down to my feet. I knew beyond the shadow of a doubt that I was healed. I knew that I would never have that sickness again, and that's exactly what happened. I've never had that problem again, not in any capacity.

Does this mean that everyone who truly receives healing from the Lord will experience a heat-like feeling go through their physical body? No, it doesn't, but some few do! We could ask the question, "Does God always heal according to our faith?" In other words, is the amount of faith we have always the barometer?

No, it isn't! While faith is certainly required, to be sure, the Lord is not sitting up in Heaven, refusing to heal us because we need five percent more faith. Such thinking is silly, but unfortunately, many preachers teach such error.

I cannot honestly answer why the Lord sometimes heals and sometimes doesn't. I cannot answer why we are prayed for several times for the same problem and receive no healing, and then seemingly out of the blue, just as the Lord did with me, prayer is answered, and we are healed.

THE LORD IS A MIRACLE WORKER

All I know is this: the Lord is still in the healing business. In fact, He is still in the miracle-working business as well! While He doesn't always heal, I thank God for the times He does heal.

While I'm on the subject, I think it might be proper to make a few statements regarding some of the modern claims that are made as it respects healing and miracles.

As should be obvious, the Lord receives no glory out of false claims. As well, the preacher pronouncing people as healed when there is no physical evidence that such has occurred, once again, doesn't bring glory to God. The problem is, almost all of these people treated thusly are, in fact, not healed.

It hurts the cause of Christ for a preacher before thousands of people to announce to that congregation that the dear soul standing before him, who, incidentally, is dying with cancer, is healed when there is, in fact, no physical proof. Almost every time, those people, at least those of my acquaintance, have died. And yet, it seems that the church asks few questions because they have been taught that to question such a preacher about such practices constitutes rebellion. In fact, it is actually taught that such individuals are above question.

NO PERSON IS ABOVE QUESTION

When preachers put themselves in such a position — and it is for certain that they have put themselves there because the Lord surely hasn't — such is a sure sign that what they are doing is not of God. Any and every believer, providing they are in a right spirit, has the scriptural right to question what is done, that is, if it doesn't seem to be proper. Any true preacher of the gospel will welcome such scrutiny.

In fact, it is my belief that being prayed for by such preachers, whomever they might be, not only doesn't help the individual in question but, in fact, can cause greater sickness.

Listen to what Paul said: *"Wherefore whosoever shall eat this bread, and drink this cup of the Lord* (the Lord's Supper), *unworthily, shall be guilty of the body and blood of the Lord.*

"But let a man examine himself, and so let him eat of that bread, and drink of that cup.

"For he who eats and drinks unworthily, eats and drinks damnation to himself, not discerning the Lord's body.

"For this cause many are weak and sickly among you, and many sleep" (I Cor. 11:27-30).

NOT PROPERLY DISCERNING THE LORD'S BODY

Paul has made some serious charges here. He has said that if we do not properly discern the Lord's body, sickness can be the result, and even premature death. Even though such a person will not lose his soul, he will definitely have his life shortened. In fact, he used the term many sleep, which should give us pause for thought.

When he spoke of believers being *"guilty of the body and blood of the Lord,"* he was meaning that such a believer was not properly *"discerning the Lord's body."*

For the believer to properly discern the Lord's body is to understand that everything he has from the Lord has come to him solely and completely through the Cross of Christ on which Jesus died.

All of this means that our faith must be exclusively in Christ and what Christ has done for us at the Cross.

HOW DOES ALL THIS TRANSLATE?

It means that if the preacher who prays for you isn't basing all that he does on the sacrifice of Christ, in other words, the Cross, he very well could be functioning with "another spirit," and, in fact, it is just about guaranteed that he is functioning accordingly (II Cor. 11:4). While thousands in the church are clamoring for some particular preacher to lay hands on them, the truth is, oftentimes, instead of bringing healing, it brings the very opposite.

Despite all of this, and we speak of the false claims, etc., the Lord is still the healer. The believer is encouraged by the Word of God to ardently seek the Lord as it regards our needs, irrespective as to what they might be, and He has promised, in His own way, to answer (Lk. 11:5-13).

TWELVE WELLS OF WATER
AND SEVENTY PALM TREES

"And they came to Elim, where were twelve wells of water, and threescore and ten palm trees: and they encamped there by the waters" (Ex.15:27).

This passage carries a spiritual significance of what was to come in the future. Even though Israel would not have seen it then, looking back, we can see it now.

First of all, the *"twelve wells of water"* spoke of the twelve apostles who would be chosen by Christ, and on which, in a sense, the new covenant would be built.

The Scripture says: *"Now therefore you are no more strangers and foreigners, but fellow citizens with the saints, and of the household of God;*

"And are built upon the foundation of the apostles and prophets, Jesus Christ Himself being the chief corner stone;

"In whom all the building fitly framed together grows unto a holy temple in the Lord:

"In whom you also are built together for a habitation of God through the Spirit" (Eph. 2:19-22).

TWELVE AND SEVENTY

The *"twelve wells of water,"* symbolizing the *"twelve apostles,"* also symbolize the government of God, for the number of government is 12. There were 12 tribes of Israel, 12 apostles, and the city, New Jerusalem, is 12,000 furlongs square. As well, it has a wall with 12 foundations, on which are written the names of the 12 apostles of the Lamb. The wall is pierced by 12 gates, with 12 angels standing at the 12 gates. As stated, 12 portrays the government of God. That government is based on apostles and prophets, whose callings continue unto this hour.

The 70 palm trees are symbolic of ministry, which must be built upon the foundation of the apostles and prophets, Jesus Christ Himself being the chief corner stone.

The Scripture tells us that Jesus *"appointed other seventy also, and sent them two and two before His face into every city and place, whither He Himself would come"* (Lk. 10:1).

Luke added to that by saying, *"And the seventy returned again with joy, saying, Lord, even the devils* (demons) *are subject unto us through Your name"* (Lk. 10:17).

THE ENCAMPMENT

The phrase, *"And they encamped there by the waters,"* signals the place in which the believer is to rest. If we pitch our tent *"there,"* so to speak, this will be according to the Word of God, and in the midst of this weary world, we will find relaxation, joy, peace, and serenity. This is that of which Jesus was speaking when He said, *"Come unto Me, all you who labor and are heavy laden, and I will give you rest"* (Mat. 11:28).

As long as the doctrine is *"Jesus Christ and Him crucified,"* which speaks of the foundation — typed by the *"twelve wells of water"* — and the ministry — typed by the *"threescore and ten palm trees"*—Christ will be found in all His glory and will be to the believer what He desires to be.

> *O listen to our wondrous story,*
> *Counted once among the lost;*
> *Yes, One came down from Heaven's glory,*
> *Saving us at awful cost!*
>
> *No angel could His place have taken,*
> *Highest of the high though He;*
> *The loved One on the Cross forsaken*
> *Was one of the Godhead three!*

Will you surrender to this Saviour?
To His scepter humbly bow?
You, too, shall come to know His favor,
He will save you, save you now.

THE
WORLD
THE
FLESH
AND THE
DEVIL

MURMURING

MURMURING

"AND THEY TOOK THEIR *journey from Elim, and all the congregation of the children of Israel came unto the wilderness of Sin, which is between Elim and Sinai, on the fifteenth day of the second month after their departing out of the land of Egypt*" (Ex. 16:1).

Verse 1 tells us that the children of Israel had been on the road exactly one month, having left Egypt the fifteenth of the first month. This indicates that they moved slowly and stopped perhaps several days at a time. About 10 or more days would bring them to Sinai.

As we shall see, Verses 2 and 3 once again proclaim the fact that the *"children of Israel murmured."* It does not take very much to cause the average person or congregation to murmur. The slightest temporary lack of water, food, clothing, money, or convenience will test the mettle of every man. Regrettably, the best will finally complain if the pressure increases beyond normal.

The *"wilderness of Sin"* between Elim — the place of the *waters,* and *Sinai,* the place of the *law* — proves a very marked and interesting position — a position of failure, no less, visited by grace.

In grace, there is no hindrance. The streams of blessing that emanate from the Lord flow onward without interruption. It is only when man puts himself under law that he forfeits everything, for then God must allow him to prove how much he can claim on the ground of his own works.

THE WILDERNESS OF SIN

It must be remembered that *"the pillar of the cloud"* led them in this direction. It was a direction that seemed to be most inhospitable. The statement, *"came unto the wilderness of Sin,"* implies that they were not quite yet in this wilderness, but near.

Concerning this position in which Israel now found herself, which was a position of difficulty, it was all a test, just as it is a test with us presently. What would Israel do? How would Israel act?

Here, for the first time, the full privation of the desert stared the people fully in the face. Every step they took was now leading them farther away from the inhabited countries and conducting them deeper into the land of desolation, and even death, or so it seemed.

The isolation of the wilderness presents the courage and faith of Moses in bringing a multitude of nearly 3 million people into such a howling waste. It demonstrates his firm confidence in the Lord God in that he, without question, would follow where the Lord did lead. And yet, some of the times would prove to be trying for him.

Moses was not ignorant of the desert and its demands. He had lived for 40 years in its immediate vicinity (Ex. 3:1), and, therefore, he knew full well that only a miracle, even a series of miracles, could meet the vast needs of such a multitude. In this, his faith was superior to that of Abraham (Gen. 12:10).

THE FIFTEENTH DAY OF THE SECOND MONTH

Why did the Holy Spirit through Moses think it significant to record the exact date as given here? As a matter of history, it seems of little interest or importance. What difference does it make to us today which month and what day of the month it was when Israel entered the wilderness of Sin?

The very fact that the Holy Spirit has recorded this detail is sufficient proof that it is not meaningless. In fact, there is nothing trivial in the Word of God. Every single word contains divine purpose and significance.

It was in the *"second month"* that they went out. In Scripture, *two* speaks of *witness* or *testimony* (Rev. 11:3). As well, it was the *"fifteenth day"* of the month. The factors of 15 are *five* and *three*. In Scripture, *five* signifies *"grace or favor"* (Gen. 43:34), and *three* is the number of *"trinity,"* hence, the number of *"manifestation,"* when life is fully manifested. By combining these definitions, we learn that God was now to give unto Israel a witness and manifestation of His grace.

In order for grace to shine forth, there must first be the dark background of sin. Grace is unmerited favor, or rather the goodness of God, and to enhance its glory, the demerits of man must be exhibited. It is *"where sin abounded, grace did much more abound"* (Rom. 5:20). Very shortly we will have an exhibition, regrettably so, of Israel's sin; but overriding this, the Lord through grace would do great and mighty things.

Now, this is not to mean, not at all, that God wills a person to sin in order that His grace may be exhibited, but grace, thank God, is available when man sins.

MURMURING

"And the whole congregation of the children of Israel murmured against Moses and Aaron in the wilderness" (Ex. 16:2).

Despite the fact of the Lord sweetening the bitter waters of Marah, pressure was now applied, and Israel responded very negatively. They *"murmured against Moses and Aaron,"* but it should be understood that if we murmur against God's man or woman, we have, in effect, murmured against God. And that's exactly the way the Lord looks at the situation. We as believers must be very careful how we speak of any believer; however, we must be especially careful how we speak of those on whom God has truly laid His hand.

Concerning this situation, Pink said, *"Here was the self-same people who had been divinely spared from the ten plagues on Egypt, who had been brought forth from the land of bondage, miraculously delivered at the Red Sea, divinely guided by a pillar of cloud and fire, day and night—now 'murmuring,' complaining, rebelling!"*

More than likely, a few began murmuring, with others picking it up, until the Scripture says that the *"whole congregation"* was murmuring against Moses and Aaron.

MURMURING, WHICH SPEAKS OF UNBELIEF, IS CONTAGIOUS

How different the scene would have been had the people begun praising God! Let the reader understand that whatever it is we do, in one way or the other, it will also be contagious. If we evidence faith, faith most definitely will be contagious. If we evidence unbelief, as stated, that too will be contagious. Whatever we do, in one way or the other, it will be contagious. If we murmur and complain, some around us will do the same. If we speak positively, some will do that as well.

While faith and praise is contagious, I'm concerned that murmuring is even far more contagious. It is somewhat like a small fire kindling a bonfire.

James said: *"And the tongue is a fire, a world of iniquity: so is the tongue among our members, that it defiles the whole body, and sets on fire the course of nature; and it is set on fire of hell. But the tongue can no man tame; it is an unruly evil, full of deadly poison. Therewith bless we God, even the Father; and therewith curse we men, which are made after the similitude of God. Out of the same mouth proceeds blessing and cursing. My brethren, these things ought not so to be. Does a fountain send forth at the same place sweet water and bitter?"* (James 3:6, 8-11).

Even though man cannot tame the tongue, which refers to such being brought to pass by one's own strength and ability, the Lord definitely can accomplish this task — but He is the only one who can!

THE CROSS

This problem — and it is a very serious problem — is to be addressed exactly as every other problem is to be addressed; that is, by understanding that our victory comes solely through the Cross, i.e., *"what Jesus did there."* It is the Holy Spirit who alone can develop proper fruit within our lives (Gal. 5:22-23).

The Holy Spirit functions within the parameters, and those parameters exclusively, of the finished work of Christ. It is all *"in Christ"* (Rom. 8:1-2).

We are obligated to do one thing, and one thing only, and that is to ever exhibit faith in Christ and His great sacrifice of Himself (Rom. 6:3-5; 8:1-2, 11; Gal. 5:5-6).

It is ever by faith, which refers to faith in Christ and His sacrifice.

Following this prescribed order, the Holy Spirit can then work grandly within our lives, bringing about the fruit of the Spirit and, thereby, making us what we ought to be in Christ. We are then the overcomer, with our *condition* being brought up to our *position*. In other words, our *state* now comes up to our *standing*.

THE OATH

"And the children of Israel said unto them, Would to God we had died by the hand of the LORD in the land of Egypt, when we sat by the flesh pots, and when we did eat bread to the full; for you have brought us forth into this wilderness, to kill this whole assembly with hunger" (Ex. 16:3).

As we read these words, we are reading an oath. This means that their sin was aggravated by an oath. They took the divine name in vain when they said that *"Would to God we had died by the hand of the LORD in the land of Egypt."*

As well, every evidence is that they lied also. As slaves of the merciless Egyptians, there is no ground whatsoever for us to suppose that they *"sat by the flesh pots"* or ate *"bread to the full."*

To accuse Moses and Aaron of bringing them into the wilderness that they might die with hunger was, in effect, as stated, accusing God. It was *Jehovah,* not simply Moses and Aaron, who had brought them forth; and He had promised that they should worship Him at Sinai (Ex. 3:12). Consequently, it was not possible then for them to die with hunger in the wilderness.

BREAD FROM HEAVEN

"Then said the LORD unto Moses, Behold, I will rain bread from heaven for you; and the people shall go out and

gather a certain rate every day, that I may prove them, whether they will walk in My law, or no" (Ex. 16:4).

As we shall later see, the murmurings of Verses 6 through 8 proclaim the fact that God hears and sees all the acts of man and will hold each person responsible as to *right* and *wrong* in every detail (I Cor. 3:11-15).

As we also shall see, the manna prefigured the descent of the True Bread, of which, if a man eat, he shall live forever (Jn. 6:51).

All of this was a test of appetite and of obedience. In Egypt, Israel had slave food; in the desert, angels' food; and the test quickly revealed that the natural man has no appetite for heavenly things.

The Holy Spirit referred to the sustenance as *"bread from Heaven."* It was a type of Christ, and the instructions given will portray how we are to address Christ.

MANNA

As the manna came from heaven, likewise, Christ, of whom it is a type, came from heaven. As bread satisfies the hunger, likewise, Christ does the same, and, in fact, Christ alone can satisfy the hunger of the soul.

Exactly as to what type of nutriments this *"bread from heaven"* contained, we aren't told; nevertheless, it provided everything the human body needed exactly as Christ provides everything the soul needs.

The people had to gather *"a certain rate every day,"* proclaiming the fact that we are to partake of Christ every day.

He is there for the taking, so to speak, and He will satisfy the longing of the soul.

Unfortunately, some people go through a ceremony or a ritual, thinking that constitutes the acceptance of Christ. It doesn't! Accepting Christ is done by faith, meaning that we accept Him as Saviour and Lord, realizing that He alone can meet our need. As we believe in what He has done for us at the Cross, He, through the power and person of the Holy Spirit, comes into our hearts and lives to abide forever (Jn. 14:16-20).

Also, the people had to go out and gather the manna, proclaiming the fact that faith must be exercised in order for Christ to be real within our lives.

PROVE THEM?

Everything the Lord does with us is to *prove us* in one way or the other.

How will we act?

How will we react?

This actually means that everything in life for the child of God is a test. We must never forget that.

Israel should have understood that it was infinitely better to be in the desert with God than in the brick kilns with Pharaoh. But no; the human heart finds it immensely difficult to give God credit for pure and perfect love. Regrettably, it has far more confidence in Satan than it does God.

Look for a moment at all the sorrow and suffering and the misery and degradation that man has endured by reason of his having hearkened to the voice of Satan. And yet, he never gives utterance to a word of complaint of his service or of desire to escape from under his hand. He is not discontented with Satan or weary of serving him. Again and again he reaps bitter fruit in those fields that Satan has thrown open to him, and yet, again and again he may be seen sowing the selfsame seed and undergoing the selfsame labors.

A SINGLE TRIFLING PRIVATION

But how different it is in reference to God! Ten thousand mercies are forgotten in the presence of a single trifling privation. He has done so much for us, which should cause us to praise Him forever, beginning right now. However, as stated, the slightest problem arises, which may, in fact, turn out to be a great blessing to us, and instead, we murmur and complain.

Nothing is more dishonoring to God than the manifestation of a complaining spirit on the part of those who belong to Him. The apostle gave it a special mark of Gentile corruption that, *"When they knew God, they glorified Him not as God, neither were thankful."* Then follows the practical result of this unthankful spirit — they became *"vain in their imaginations, and their foolish heart was darkened"* (Rom. 1:21).

This means that the heart that ceases to retain a thankful sense of God's goodness will speedily become dark.

For Israel to know and understand the meaning and supply of this heavenly food, they needed a heart that was weaned from Egypt's influences. This had to be for them to be satisfied with or enjoy *"bread from heaven."*

MODERN BELIEVERS

While the believer must be in the world, we are definitely not to be of the world.

John plainly told us that the world is our enemy. He said: *"Love not the world, neither the things that are in the world. If any man love the world, the love of the Father is not in him. For all that is in the world, the lust of the flesh, and the lust of the eyes, and the pride of life, is not of the Father, but is of the world."*

And then, *"And the world passes away, and the lust thereof: but he who does the will of God abides forever"* (I Jn. 2:15-17).

At least one of the greatest sins of the church is the use of the world in order to attract people. What they seemingly fail to realize is, it doesn't matter how many are attracted in this fashion, none will be drawn to the Lord. The Holy Spirit, as should be obvious, doesn't use the world, or anything in the world as far as its spirit is concerned, to draw men to Christ. In fact, as stated, the moment the spirit of the world is engaged, the Holy Spirit closes the door.

THE TWO METHODS OF DESTRUCTION
REGARDING THE CHURCH

The first method that Satan uses is to stop the preacher from preaching the Cross. With that done, he knows that the Christian is, for all practical purposes, defenseless. Regrettably, Satan has been successful in virtually closing down the preaching of the Cross. As a result, the church doesn't know where it's been, where it is, or where it's going. In fact, since the Reformation, it's never been in worse condition than it is now.

Second, the spirit of the world in the music being presented by many, if not most, churches is completely destroying the young people, who are supposed to be the church of tomorrow.

What type of spiritual climate is it whenever scores of church buses line up in front of a nightclub in order for the kids to hear some so-called Christian rock group when, in reality, they are Christian just about as much as I am president of the United States.

It's hard to blame the kids for this abomination, and abomination it is. The preachers are to be blamed. In fact, the modern church is exactly like Israel of old, *"sheep without a shepherd."*

GENERATION OF VIPERS

For preachers to expose their kids to such demon-inspired direction is the same as feeding poison to an individual. In fact, it's worse because it will not only cause physical wreckage but the loss of the soul as well.

Jesus called such spiritual leaders *"snakes."* He said, *"You serpents, you generation of vipers, how can you escape the damnation of hell?"* (Mat. 23:33).

So, the Devil has succeeded in pulling the church away from the Cross, which makes it very easy to introduce the spirit of the world, which he has very successfully done.

To mix the world with Christ will not work, as mixing Egypt with Israel would not work. In fact, the Lord purposely took them into the wilderness in order that all remnants of Egypt would be purged from them. Even then, the problem persisted of the children of Israel desiring to go back to Egypt, which seemed to be their response to most problems.

Can you imagine desiring to go back to slavery! But that continues to be the problem of the human race.

The Lord must *"prove them"* in order to see whether they would walk in His law or not. Regrettably, they didn't, and that generation perished in the wilderness.

THE SIXTH DAY

"And it shall come to pass, that on the sixth day they shall prepare that which they bring in; and it shall be twice as much as they gather daily" (Ex. 16:5).

The period of seven days was known to the children of Israel as a week, which appeared in the story of Jacob and Laban (Gen. 29:27).

There is little or no record that they called their days by specific names as we do presently, but rather by numbers. So, it seems that the week actually began with the first day that the manna was given. On the seventh day, the Lord instituted the Sabbath, which we will find later in this chapter.

It seems that they were to gather twice as much on the sixth day as they had done on the previous days, which the Lord would miraculously multiply in order that they may have sustenance the next day, on which they would not be allowed to do any work.

This tells us that Christ, the true Bread of Life, will be enough for us, not only during the normal times but, as well, during times when it seems as though He has sent no provision. He has, in fact, sent enough provision for all, irrespective of the need.

As the manna also had some type of miracle quality, as stated, which could cause it to multiply or diminish, irrespective as to what was gathered, likewise, Christ is to the person exactly as He ought to be. He is the giver of miracles and will perform graciously and constantly for all believers, at least those who will stand upon His promises, or else, He can withhold blessings.

THE GLORY OF THE LORD

"And Moses and Aaron said unto all the children of Israel, At evening, then you shall know that the LORD has brought you out from the land of Egypt: And in the morning, then you shall see the glory of the LORD; for that He

hears your murmurings against the LORD: *and what are we, that you murmur against us?"* (Ex. 16:6-7).

The evening of which Moses spoke here when he said, *"then you shall know,"* probably refers to the descent of the quails. Moses must have received a distinct intimation of the coming arrival of the quails, though he had not yet recorded it. In fact, it seems that he seldom recorded both the divine message and his delivery of it. In general, he placed upon record either the message only or its delivery only.

While they could see the arrival of the quails in the evening, the next morning, they would see the manna. All of this is referred to as the *"glory of the* LORD.*"*

THE EVENING AND THE MORNING

In fact, Israel, in Bible times, counted their day as beginning at about 6 p.m., with the evening being the beginning and the morning, beginning at about 6 a.m., being the ending, the very opposite of our present view. Now our new day begins at midnight. In fact, that's the way the Lord described it in the Genesis, Chapter 1, account, *"And the evening and the morning were the first day"* (Gen. 1:5).

Moses attempted to impress upon the people that their murmurings against him and Aaron were actually against the Lord. He asked the question, *"What are we, that you murmur against us?"*

In essence, he was saying, *"What power have we of our own? We have no hereditary rank, no fixed definite posi-*

tion. We are simply the leaders whom you have chosen to follow because you believed us to have a commission from God. Apart from this, we are nobodies. But, if our commission is conceded, we are to you in the place of God, and to murmur against us is to murmur against Jehovah."

MURMURINGS

"And Moses said, This shall be, when the LORD shall give you in the evening flesh to eat, and in the morning bread to the full; for that the LORD hears your murmurings which you murmur against Him: and what are we? your murmurings are not against us, but against the LORD.

"And Moses spoke unto Aaron, Say unto all the congregation of the children of Israel, Come near before the LORD: for He has heard your murmurings" (Ex. 16:8-9).

Verse 8 is basically a repetition of Verse 7, but it emphasizes the statements of that verse and prepares the way for what follows.

When looking back toward Egypt, Israel murmured; when looking forward toward the wilderness, they saw the glory of the Lord.

Discontent magnifies what is past and vilifies what is present without regard to truth or reason. The absurd then murmurs!

The Lord takes notice of the people's complaints. As a God of pity, He took cognizance of their necessity, which was the occasion of their murmuring. As a just and holy God, He took cognizance of their base and unworthy reflections upon His servant Moses and was much displeased with them. When we begin to fret and to be uneasy, we ought to consider that God hears all of our murmurings, though silent or only the murmurings of the heart.

Those in positions of leadership do not hear all the murmurs of those whom they are attempting to lead. It is well that we do not, perhaps because we could not bear it. But God hears, and yet, bears.

We must not think that because God does not immediately take vengeance on men for their sins, therefore, He does not notice them. He heard the murmurings of Israel and was grieved with that generation, and yet, continued His care of them as the tender parent of a froward child.

THE CLOUD

"And it came to pass, as Aaron spoke unto the whole congregation of the children of Israel, that they looked toward the wilderness, and, behold, the glory of the LORD appeared in the cloud" (Ex. 16:10).

Verse 10 seems to indicate that the Lord had commanded Moses that the entirety of the children of Israel should present themselves as a *"whole congregation"* to the Lord, hence, the appearance of the Lord to the congregation in the cloud.

The Scripture says that *"they looked toward the wilderness,"* which means that they were on the edge of that vast wasteland. But yet, the wilderness was where the *"LORD appeared in the cloud."*

Wherever the Lord is, that's where I want to be. Of course, we now realize that due to the Cross, the Lord, through the person of the Holy Spirit, is with us constantly. In fact, Jesus said of Him, *"And I will pray the Father, and He shall give you another Comforter* (Helper), *that He may abide with you forever"* (Jn. 14:16).

However, I'm not speaking here of His abiding, but rather His work, that is, what He is doing in this world, and especially His plan for me. God has a special plan for every single believer. He has a special place and a special work cut out for that particular individual. Accordingly, His presence will lead me.

PERSONAL TESTIMONY

The Lord has led me in this capacity all of my life and ministry. In 1968, He told me to go on radio with a daily program, 15 minutes in length, which we called *The Campmeeting Hour.* We were soon on some 600 stations daily, with the largest daily audience in the nation as it referred to gospel. In 1972, the Lord told me to go on television and even told me how the program was to be structured. About two or three years after making our debut on television, which was not easy to say the least, the Lord told me to begin translating the program from English into various languages. This we did, ultimately airing the gospel through television in many countries of the world.

The Lord told me, even as He led me, to take our meetings from the churches into the large auditoriums and coliseums, which we did. He also instructed me regarding citywide and even nationwide meetings in foreign countries, which we also carried out. We saw literally hundreds of thousands, and I exaggerate not, brought to a saving knowledge of Jesus Christ.

In the first part of 1999, He led me, as well, to begin SonLife Radio by acquiring stations all over this nation, which we have done and continue to do even unto this hour. Someone asked me the other day why we didn't do the same thing with television stations. My answer was immediate: The Lord hasn't told me to do that!

As it regards SonLife Radio, the Lord told me exactly how to structure the programming and how to acquire the stations even though we had no money.

A TELEVISION NETWORK

In 1997, in answer to soul-searching prayer — which, in fact, had lasted on a daily basis for the previous six years — the Lord began to open up to me the Message of the Cross, which changed my life and ministry. To be sure, it was not new but actually that which He had given to the Apostle Paul so long ago. And yet, this message has been all but lost to the modern church. That is beyond tragedy, if such a thing could be, considering that this message is the very foundation of the gospel (Rom. 6:1-14; 8:1-11; I Cor. 1:17-18, 21, 23; 2:2; Eph. 2:13-18; Col. 2:14-15).

So, what am I trying to say? I'm saying that if we are to have the presence of the Lord in our lives and ministry, we must be where He wants us to be, even if it looks like a wilderness. Where the presence of the Lord actually is has nothing to do with my likes or dislikes. In other words, I only want and desire to be where He is and to be in the midst of what He is doing, wherever that location might be.

In 2010, the Lord did something totally unexpected. He told me to begin a television network, which would broadcast the gospel 24 hours a day, seven days a week. He also told me that I was to use only preachers from this ministry in order that the message, actually, the Message of the Cross, would be the same. We immediately set out to do what He told us to do.

At the time of this dictation, we now go into 72 million homes in the U.S.A., broadcasting 24 hours a day, seven days a week. We are also airing in some 150 million homes outside of the U.S., plus the programming is available to some 2 billion people over the Internet. In fact, the network is growing faster than any network in history, secular or otherwise. We give the Lord the praise and the glory.

THE LORD SPOKE

"And the LORD spoke unto Moses, saying" (Ex. 16:11).
Past miracles are convincing, but unless there are fresh evidences of God, the natural man will soon forget and lapse into unbelief again.

We will later see in Verses 13 through 20 the miracle of the quails and the manna. The manna prefigured the descent of the True Bread, of which, if a man eats, he shall live forever (Jn. 6:51).

In Egypt, Israel had slave food; in the desert, angel's food. The test quickly revealed that the natural man has little appetite for heavenly things, for the people soon called it *"light food."*

The manna, as we shall see, was so precious that it could not bear contact with the earth. It fell upon the dew and had to be gathered before the sun came up. This teaches us that yesterday's blessings will not do for today or today's blessings for tomorrow. Thus must the Christian feed upon Christ as He reveals Himself in the Scriptures.

Israel in the desert presented a striking picture! Egypt was behind them, Canaan was before them, the wilderness was around them, and the manna was above them. Every time they looked back toward Egypt, they murmured; when looking forward toward the wilderness, they saw the glory of the Lord. The manna was a type of Christ as well as a type of the Word of God.

LEADING AND GUIDANCE FROM THE LORD?

A preacher told me the other day — speaking of one of the largest religious denominations in the world, of which he was actually a part — that they did not believe that the Lord spoke to people in this day and age. In other words, they do not believe in any leading or guidance from the Lord, relying instead on common sense, etc. They claim that the Word of God is the only instruction that we need, and that when the

Word was completed with the book of Revelation, the Lord ceased to speak to anyone.

While it is certainly true that the Lord will not take away or add to His Word, and everything He says will definitely coincide with the Word, still, every indication is given in the Word of God that the Lord continues to lead His people with personal direction, even as I have been relating. As we gave regarding commentary on the previous verse, the Lord has led me all of my life, and He has done so by speaking to my heart.

In fact, He speaks to me through His Word, through songs (which always coincide with His Word), through dreams and visions, and through impressions upon my spirit, as well as gifts of the Spirit (I Cor. 12:8-10).

No! The Lord didn't quit speaking to His people in the giving of direction when the canon of Scripture was completed as it regards the book of Revelation. Such a thought, to be frank, is absurd! However, I will hasten to say again:

The Lord is not adding to His Word or taking from His Word. Anything He gives to anyone will always coincide with His Word. If it doesn't, it's not from the Lord.

I HAVE HEARD

"I have heard the murmurings of the children of Israel: speak unto them, saying, At evening you shall eat flesh, and in the morning you shall be filled with bread; and you shall know that I am the LORD your God" (Ex. 16:12).

The Lord pointedly told Israel that He had heard their murmurings. Let it be understood that this was the first sin that was committed by Israel after being delivered from Egyptian bondage. We should take a lesson from this.

More than likely, that is the besetting sin of most Christians presently. To murmur in any capacity, which refers to complaining and finding fault, is, in essence, a complaint against God. In effect, we are telling Him that we can do a better job than He is doing, which shows gross spiritual ignorance, and at the same time, portrays the fact that we aren't very thankful for all of the wonderful things the Lord has done for us. To be sure, He has done much!

As we've already stated, you very seldom hear the children of the Devil complaining about the Devil. If they complain at all, it's that they are not able to serve him more and better, whether they understand such or not. However, we Christians are very quick to complain about God. The truth is, most Christians don't realize that what they are saying is actually against God, but to be sure, that's exactly what it is.

GRACE

Despite their murmurings, grace overruled, exactly as grace overrules our actions many times, and presented the children of Israel with a miracle of tremendous proportions — manna from heaven in the mornings and quail at night.

However, let it ever be understood that despite the factor of grace, if the murmuring continues, even as it did with

Israel, ultimately, the Lord will take a hand, and chastisement will be the result.

We are seeing here the unbelief of Israel, which would ultimately result in the adult generation dying in the wilderness and being refused admittance into the land of Canaan. It all began with murmuring. As stated, let that be a lesson to us.

THE QUAILS

"And it came to pass, that at evening the quails came up, and covered the camp: and in the morning the dew lay round about the host" (Ex. 16:13).

As it appears by the subsequent narrative, it seems that the quails were supplied, not regularly, but only on rare occasions. In fact (so far as appears), they were only supplied here in the wilderness of Sin and at Kibroth-hattaavah in the wilderness of Paran (Num. 11:31-34). One might say that they were not a necessity, but rather an indulgence.

The mention of the dew in this manner implies that which looked like dew and was in part dew, but not wholly so. The next verse explains it to a greater degree.

Concerning the quails, they regularly migrated from Syria and Arabia in the autumn and wintered in the interior of Africa when they then returned northward in immense masses in the spring. When these birds approach the coast after a long flight over the Red Sea, they are often so exhausted that they fall to the ground and then settle. They are then easily taken by the hand or killed with sticks. Their flesh is regarded by the natives as a delicacy.

At any rate, the Lord would have had to perform a miracle to bring this about in that the quail had to land at exactly the place where the children of Israel were encamped. As well, there must have been at least 10 million to 20 million quails to satisfy the hunger of some 3 million Israelites.

MANNA

"And when the dew that lay was gone up, behold, upon the face of the wilderness there lay a small round thing, as small as the hoar frost on the ground.

"And when the children of Israel saw it, they said one to another, It is manna: for they didn't know what it was. And Moses said unto them, This is the bread which the LORD has given you to eat" (Ex. 16:14-15).

It is only as we feed upon Christ Himself that we truly feed upon the written Word, and no one can properly understand Christ unless one properly understands His mission, which was the Cross. If we do not understand Christ in this fashion, hence, Paul saying, *"We preach Christ crucified"* (I Cor. 1:23), then, in effect, we will be attending *"another Jesus"* (II Cor. 11:4).

Let me make the statement simpler: To properly understand the Word of God, we must, at the same time, properly understand the Cross. While everything that Jesus did was of immense significance, as should be overly obvious, it is always the Cross that must be the chief emphasis. That's why the apostle said, *"For Christ sent me not to baptize, but to preach the gospel: not with wisdom of words, lest the Cross of Christ should be made of none effect"* (I Cor. 1:17).

A MODERN NARRATIVE

Concerning this, Pink says:

"Beneath many a figure and behind innumerable shadows and symbols the anointed eye may discern the glories of our blessed Lord. It should be our chief delight as we read the Old Testament Scriptures, to prayerfully search for that which foreshadows Him of whom 'Moses and the prophets' did write. All doubt is removed as to whether or not the manna pointed to the incarnate Son by His own words in John 6:32-33. There we find the Saviour saying: *'Verily, verily, I say unto you, Moses gave you not that bread from heaven; but My Father gives you the True Bread from heaven. For the Bread of God is He which comes down from heaven and gives life unto the world.'"*

So, we will take this occasion, as it regards the manna, to portray Christ in this sign and symbol of so long ago.

THE GIVING OF THE MANNA

The manna was given to Israel because of great need; likewise, Jesus came to this world simply because it was lost and in great need. In fact, if not for His coming, the world would have been eternally lost.

Did man deserve this, the giving of the manna? The answer can be easily ascertained by asking the question, as well, of Israel. No, Israel didn't deserve the manna, and the world didn't deserve Christ, as we don't deserve anything that's good either.

What does the Scripture say?

"But God, who is rich in mercy, for His great love where-with He loved us,

"Even when we were dead in sins, has quickened us together (made us spiritually alive) with Christ, (by grace you are saved;)

"And has raised us up together, and made us sit together in heavenly places in Christ Jesus:

"That in the ages to come He might show the exceed-ing riches of His grace in His kindness toward us through Christ Jesus" (Eph. 2:4-7).

GRACE

I get amazed at times at Christians who have been taught wrong, who claim that a person forfeits grace if he does something wrong. If that, in fact, is the case, then no person can be saved. The truth is, the person who has done wrong, which includes every human being who has ever lived, is the one who desperately needs grace and the one to whom grace is given, that is, if he functions according to God's way.

And what is that way?

The believer must confess his sin before the Lord, which can be done in a moment's time. He must sincerely and truly want to lay such wrongdoing aside and, thereby, ask for the grace of God to do so. Grace is simply the goodness of God extended to undeserving people. Grace doesn't mean that God overlooks sin or condones it; quite the contrary is true. Grace simply means that the Lord will forgive if the person confesses his or her sin, and does so with sincerity. If any individual thinks he can do anything he desires, no matter how bad it is — with him continuing with his sinning — and grace will guarantee its forgiveness, he will never be given grace on such grounds.

FALLING FROM GRACE

For a believer to fall from grace, which Paul mentions in Galatians 5:4, that Christian has to trust in things other than the Cross. All grace comes exclusively through the finished work of Christ and our faith in that finished work, which enables the Holy Spirit to carry out His work within our lives. If our faith is transferred from the Cross to other things, irrespective as to what those other things are, we fall from grace, as should be obvious (Gal. 2:21; 5:4).

No, it was the grace of God, and certainly not their good works, that occasioned the manna for Israel. It is the same for us presently.

A PERSONAL EXPERIENCE

Sometime back, I remember watching two preachers over television discuss grace. Their summation was that if anyone did something wrong, then the grace of God was completely lifted from that person, in other words, they were doomed. They had fallen from grace, at least according to these two preachers.

The truth is, these two preachers were trusting things other than the Cross of Christ, which means that they themselves were fallen from grace. The idea that if someone does something wrong, then he forfeits grace, is ridiculous. As stated, if that is the case, then every believer is fallen from grace. No, to have the grace of God come to us in an uninterrupted flow, we simply must anchor our faith in Christ and what He has done for us at the Cross. That being done and maintained, the grace of God will always flow to such an individual in an unending supply.

THE PLACE WHERE THE MANNA FELL

The manna fell in the wilderness; likewise, this world is a wilderness. In fact, the place where the manna fell was actually called *"the wilderness of Sin"* (Ex. 16:1).

Likewise, to this *"wilderness of Sin,"* which we refer to as the world, did Jesus come.

When He came, He exposed the hidden things of darkness! The response of both Jews and Gentiles to His *"light"* was to murder Him. Darkness, in fact, hates light.

THE GLORY OF THE LORD WAS LINKED
WITH THE GIVING OF THE MANNA

In Verse 10, it tells us that *"the glory of the Lord appeared in the cloud,"* as it concerned Israel. This is the first time we read of the appearing of that glory. Then the manna was given.

Not until the Son of God became incarnate was *"the glory of the Lord"* fully revealed. But then, when the eternal Word became flesh and lived among men, then as the beloved apostle declares, *"We beheld His glory, the glory as of the only begotten of the Father"* (Jn. 1:14). In fact, the *"glory of God"* is seen *"in the face of Jesus Christ"* (II Cor. 4:6).

THE MANNA CAME DOWN FROM HEAVEN

The manna was not a product of the earth or anything that man could do. It was exclusively a product of heaven.

In fact, God said to Moses, *"Behold, I will rain bread from heaven for you."*

This manna had nothing to do with human ability or human skill. It descended strictly from God. It was a gift from Heaven to this sinful world, this *"wilderness of Sin."*

As well, our Lord wasn't a product of this earth, even though He was incarnate — God became man by being born of a woman, but with man having no part to play whatsoever.

The Scripture says, *"The first man* (Adam) *is of the earth, earthy: the second Man* (Jesus Christ) *is the Lord from heaven"* (I Cor. 15:47).

THE MANNA WAS A FREE GIFT FROM GOD

Israel did not earn this manna and, in fact, could not earn the manna. It was solely and completely a free gift from God. In fact, God has nothing for sale, and even if He did, there would be no way that you and I could come by the purchase price. But Jesus totally and completely paid the price for us.

I suppose the most oft quoted Scripture from the Bible amply explains this of what I say, *"For God so loved the world, that He gave His only begotten Son, that whosoever believes in Him should not perish, but have everlasting life"* (Jn. 3:16).

Paul referred to the giving of Christ as *"God's unspeakable gift"* (II Cor. 9:15).

THE MANNA WAS SENT TO ISRAEL ONLY

The manna was God's provision for His elect people, and for none other. We do not read of the Lord raining manna upon the Egyptians or the Canaanites, or anyone else for that matter. It was given to Israel in the wilderness, and to them alone. Likewise, Christ is God's provision for believers only. The unredeemed cannot have Christ, cannot know Christ, cannot experience Christ, and, therefore, cannot have His blessings. That is for the redeemed only.

Secondly, this manna was sent to a needy people, as should be obvious. Likewise, Christ is sent to a needy world, and for those who accept Him, He will be all that we need.

In fact, the man cannot be complete until he knows *the Man*, the Lord Jesus Christ (Col. 2:10).

Let's say it another way: A person cannot even remotely be a whole person until that person knows the Lord. Only then can such a one reach toward the level of what God intended for a human being to be.

THE MANNA CAME TO WHERE
THE ISRAELITES WERE

We talk about people finding the Lord.

The truth is, the Lord found the people. In fact, man, being spiritually dead, cannot in any way find the Lord or anything of the Lord unless the Lord purposely reveals Himself to such a person, which He definitely did to all who are presently saved.

God does not tamper with the will. It is still *"whosoever will,"* and that will never change (Rev. 22:17; Jn. 3:16).

As the gospel is preached, and the Holy Spirit anoints the Word, He, at the same time, strikes conviction to the hearts of the unbelievers. This is when their will is brought into play. They can either accept or reject. Sadly, most, it seems, reject the Lord.

However, if they accept the Lord, which all do by their free will, to be sure, the Lord will accept them.

The Scripture says, *"All who the Father gives Me shall come to Me; and him who comes to Me I will in no wise cast out"* (Jn. 6:37).

THE MANNA GATHERED BY EACH INDIVIDUAL

The Lord said, *"Gather of it every man according to his eating"* (Vs. 16).

Receiving Christ is always a personal matter. No one can receive Christ for someone else. The individual in question must make the decision himself. There is no such thing as salvation by proxy.

So, this means that the Mormons cannot transfer someone to heaven who has already died but did not know the Lord. In fact, with the Mormon doctrine being totally unbiblical, there is no Mormon who is saved.

Likewise, it is not possible for Catholics to get a person out of purgatory, which, incidentally, doesn't even exist.

All salvation is on this side of the grave. There are no opportunities after death. The Scripture says the gospel of Christ is *"the power of God unto salvation to every one who believes"* (Rom. 1:16), and the Scripture further says, *"He who believes not shall be damned"* (Mk. 16:16).

So, salvation is strictly a personal matter, and a personal matter alone. Each individual has to have his own experience with Christ. Paul said, *"Who (Christ) loved me, and gave Himself for me"* (Gal. 2:20).

THE MANNA MET A DAILY NEED

The manna gathered today would not suffice for tomorrow. They needed to obtain a fresh supply each day.

This is where many believers miss the mark. They do not understand that it is imperative that we feast on Christ each and every day. Christ Himself said, *"Give us this day our daily bread."* While such *"daily bread"* can be looked at as a daily sustenance regarding our physical and material needs, it also speaks of Christ, who is the Bread of Life.

THE APPETITE DETERMINED
THE AMOUNT GATHERED

How true this is of the believer as it regards Christ. We all have as much of Christ as we desire, no more and no less. If our desire is large, and we open our mouths wide, He will fill them.

The Scripture says that the children of Israel gathered the manna, *"some more, some less"* (Vss. 16-17). So, the appetite governed the amount gathered.

THE MANNA WAS DESPISED BY THOSE
WHO DID NOT BELONG TO THE LORD

The Scripture points out the mixed multitude who was among the children of Israel, which consisted of Egyptians who had come out with them. Some of the children of Israel joined with the Egyptians in criticizing the manna (Num. 11:4-6).

The person who is losing his way with God is primarily losing his way simply because he doesn't understand his need for Christ.

Mostly, the reason for that pertains to the believer trusting things other than Christ and Him crucified. As a result, he is committing *"spiritual adultery"* (Rom. 7:1-4), which, as would be understood, cools one's love for Christ. This is the *"lukewarm"* situation that Jesus mentioned in one of His messages to the seven churches of Asia (Rev. 3:15-16).

I am persuaded that a failure of the believer to understand the Cross and how it refers and plays into one's sanctification is the crowning sin of the church. It is the cause of all problems, and I mean all problems.

THE MANNA FELL UPON THE DEW, NOT UPON THE DUST OF THE GROUND

Dust speaks of fallen man and calls attention to the corruption that sin has worked in him (Gen. 3:19). So, the manna, typifying Christ, fell not upon *"the dust,"* but rather upon *"the dew."* The dew is a type of the Holy Spirit, which characterized Christ. He was anointed with the oil of gladness above all His fellows (Ps. 45:7). He said of Himself, *"The Spirit of the Lord is upon Me, because He has anointed Me"* (Lk. 4:18).

He did not come down here to share our corrupt nature, for that would have done no good. He came to get us out from under the dominance of this corrupt nature, and did so by His finished work at the Cross (Col. 2:14-15).

He took upon Himself the form of a servant, but the body that was prepared for Him (Heb. 10:5) belonged not to the *"dust"* of this earth, but was rather a product of the Holy Spirit (Lk. 1:35).

Let's say it another way: He was not the product of Joseph's sperm or Mary's egg. Mary merely furnished a house for the gestation period before the birth of Christ. In fact, Jesus did not carry Joseph or Mary's features in any manner.

THE MANNA WAS WHITE IN COLOR

As we will later study, the Scripture says, *"And the house of Israel called the name thereof manna: and it was like coriander seed, white"* (Ex. 16:31).

As should be obvious, this speaks of the spotless purity of our Lord, not only in His person, but, as well, as it was manifested outwardly in His daily walk. He *"knew no sin"* (II Cor. 5:21). He was *"without sin"* (Heb. 4:15). He *"did no sin"* (I Pet. 2:22). He was *"holy, harmless, undefiled, separate from sinners"* (Heb. 7:26).

In I Peter, we are told that He was a Lamb without spot and without blemish (I Pet. 1:19). The former expression refers to the absence of outward pollution, while the latter refers to the absence of inward defect.

Pink says, "In His walk through this scene of corruption He contracted no defilement. He alone could touch the leper without being contaminated. He was 'without spot,' pure, white."

This completely lays aside the teaching that Christ became a sinner on the Cross, died as a sinner, and, thereby, went to the burning side of hell, where He was *"born again"* three days later and then resurrected. There is nothing in the Bible as it concerns such teaching. In fact, this teaching, the Jesus Died Spiritually doctrine, shifts redemption from the Cross to hell itself, which, of course, is preposterous. Jesus died physically, which was the penalty for our sin; He did not die spiritually (I Pet. 3:18).

THE MANNA WAS SWEET TO THE TASTE

"The taste of it was like wafers made with honey" (Ex. 16:31).

The Scripture says, *"As the apple tree among the trees of the wood, so is my beloved among the sons. I sat down under his shadow with great delight, and his fruit was sweet to my taste"* (Song of Sol. 2:3).

The word *sweet,* which the manna typified, is a beautiful description of Christ. David said, *"O taste and see that the* LORD *is good"* (Ps. 34:8).

Living for Christ, which refers to association and relationship with Christ, is the most wonderful, the most glorious, and the most fulfilled life that one could ever know. In fact, there is no way for life to be what it ought to be, not even remotely so, without Christ.

Unfortunately, with the unredeemed world being spiritually dead, it doesn't know this. In fact, it has no conception of what it is to live for God, and cannot have until it is born again.

But truly, the manna, which is a type of Christ, being sweet is a beautiful and apt description.

THE MANNA WAS GROUND AND BAKED

The Scripture says concerning the manna, they *"ground it in mills, or beat it in a mortar, and baked it in pans, and made cakes of it"* (Num. 11:8).

This speaks of the sufferings of our blessed Lord!

We sometimes erroneously think that Christ was never tempted. In fact, He was tempted to a far greater degree by Satan than we would ever be tempted. The Scripture actually says He *"was in all points tempted like as we are, yet without sin"* (Heb. 4:15).

Others claim that while He may have been tempted, He, in fact, could not have succumbed to the temptation. They base their conclusion on the fact that Jesus is God, and God cannot sin.

Jesus is God. In fact, He never ceased to be God, even when He became man. As one Greek scholar put it, and rightly so, *"In the incarnation, He laid aside His expression of deity, while never losing His possession of deity."* And yes, in this particular capacity, He could have failed. Otherwise, the temptations would have made no sense. Even more so, to be the last Adam, which He was, He had to be subject to failure exactly as the first Adam, or else, He would not have fulfilled the type (I Cor. 15:45-50).

THE DEITY OF CHRIST

The argument of His deity is easily proven. Even though Jesus definitely was God, He also grew hungry and tired just like any other human being. We know that God cannot be hungry or tired, but, as stated, He laid aside the expression of His deity although never losing its possession. The Scripture says of Him, *"He is despised and rejected of men; a man of sorrows, and acquainted with grief: and we hid as it were our faces from Him; He was despised, and we esteemed Him not"* (Isa. 53:3).

As the last Adam and the second Man, He suffered all things that we should have suffered, and yet, never failed in even the slightest degree. As our representative Man, the second Man, He did what we could not do for ourselves. As our substitute, He did bear the penalty that we should have borne but couldn't.

THE MANNA WAS PRESERVED ON THE SABBATH

The Sabbath was a type of the rest we have in Christ. It was not a day of so-called worship, but rather a day of rest. It was meant to typify what Christ would do for us when He came. That's why Jesus said, *"Come unto Me, all you who labor and are heavy laden, and I will give you rest"* (Mat. 11:28).

If the manna was kept over till the next day, normally it would breed worms and stink. This was done so by the Lord because He didn't want Israel gathering the manna, except for the needs of that particular day; however, on the Sabbath, this did not happen. Whatever manna was left over would be perfectly fresh on the Sabbath morning, even though that was not the case on the other mornings of the week.

WE REST IN CHRIST

The idea is, as stated, Christ is our *rest*. But what does that mean? It means the struggle is over. Normal Christianity is for us to place our faith exclusively in Christ and what He has done for us at the Cross, which will then give latitude to the Holy Spirit to work mightily within our lives. Then, without fight or struggle, the fruit of the Spirit will be developed within us, and victory on a perpetual basis will be ours (Rom. 8:1-11).

I know what it is to not understand the Cross as it refers to sanctification and to, thereby, try to make myself holy or righteous. My labors were all in vain. It's like a man in quicksand. The more he struggles, the deeper he gets.

But when I learned through revelation what Christ has done for me at the Cross and how it affects my sanctification, i.e., my everyday life and living before God, I then learned what *"more abundant life"* actually means (Jn. 10:10). Without strife and without struggle, I found victory to be mine. It was due totally and completely to my faith in Christ and what He has done for me regarding His finished work. That's why Paul bluntly said, *"For in Jesus Christ neither circumcision avails anything, nor uncircumcision; but faith which works by love"* (Gal. 5:6).

THE MANNA WAS LAID UP BEFORE THE LORD

The high priest of the old Judaic economy entered into the Holy of Holies once a year and there offered up blood on the mercy seat, which was to atone for himself and Israel. It was all a type of what Christ would do when He, in fact, did come.

Well, Christ has come, has gone to the Cross, and has shed His precious blood. However, He did not enter into the Holy of Holies as the Aaronic high priest, but rather *"into heaven itself, now to appear in the presence of God for us"* (Heb. 9:24).

There is no record that He offered up blood on the mercy seat of heaven because had He done that, it would mean that the Cross of Calvary did not produce a finished work. However, we know that it did produce a finished work simply because Jesus said, *"It is finished"* (Jn. 19:30).

His presence before God means that God has accepted fully His sacrifice of Himself, and His appearance at the very presence of God, i.e., the throne of God, guarantees that work (Heb. 1:3).

The golden pot in which the manna was preserved tells of how God is glorified in Him whom it foreshadowed.

THE MANNA IS CALLED ANGELS' FOOD

The psalmist said, *"Man did eat angels' food: He sent them meat to the full"* (Ps. 78:25).

Christ not only feeds the souls of those of His people who are upon earth, but He also satisfies the hearts of celestial beings. The unfallen angels find their chief delight in feeding upon Christ. They worship Him, they serve Him, and they tell forth His praises. There are several passages in the book of Revelation that proclaim this fact (Rev. 6:11-14).

THE MANNA WAS GIVEN IN THE NIGHT

During the hours of darkness, the manna fell. This is typical of the darkness of spiritual night, which had settled over the earth when Jesus came. As well, it has settled over every unbeliever, and only by the Light being shown, which Light is Christ, can such a person be brought from darkness to light.

In fact, the worst night of all is just ahead when the Antichrist will make his debut for world leadership, and for awhile, it will look like he will succeed. But at the darkest time when Israel is pressed, and it looks like she will be totally destroyed, even with the Antichrist having taken half of Jerusalem, then the Lord of Glory will come back, and will do so with healing in His wings. He will come back crowned *"King of kings and Lord of lords."* Then, for the first time in human history, the light of Jesus Christ and all of His glory will fill the earth.

THE MANNA IS NOW HIDDEN

"To him who overcomes will I give to eat of the hidden manna" (Rev. 2:17). This speaks of Christ.

Unseen by the eye of nature, He remains in heaven till that day when He shall be manifested before the entire world.

The Lord Jesus Christ is coming back!

The Scripture says:

"And when He had spoken these things, while they beheld, He was taken up; and a cloud received Him out of their sight.

"And while they looked steadfastly toward Heaven as He went up, behold, two men stood by them in white apparel;

"Which also said, You men of Galilee, why do you stand gazing up into heaven? this same Jesus, which is taken up from you into heaven, shall so come in like manner as you have seen Him go into heaven" (Acts 1:9-11).

Due to the fact that He is now *"hidden,"* the world scoffs at His return; but irrespective of that, the Lord of Glory is going to come back to this world, and then, and only then, will it know peace.

What we've tried to say as it regards the manna being a type of Christ, we realize is woefully inadequate. But again, who can do justice to our Lord? However, perhaps we've said some things that will be a blessing to you.

THE COMMAND OF THE LORD

"This is the thing which the LORD has commanded, Gather of it every man according to his eating, an omer for every man, according to the number of your persons; take you every man for them which are in his tents.

"And the children of Israel did so, and gathered, some more, some less.

"And when they did mete it with an omer, he who gathered much had nothing over, and he who gathered little had no lack; they gathered every man according to his eating" (Ex. 16:16-18).

As should be understood from the text, all of this was very personal. First of all, as Verse 16 proclaims, this given is a command of the Lord.

It says, *"An omer for every man."*

An omer is the equivalent of six pints. Considering there were approximately 3 million people, this would play out to some 18 million pints, or about 13.5 million pounds gathered daily. To help us understand it even more, it would take a train pulling 45 cars, with each car having in it 15 tons, to take care of one day's supply. This means that approximately 2 million tons of manna were gathered annually by Israel. Let it be remembered that this continued for nearly 40 years!

THE COMMAND WAS EMPHATIC

"And Moses said, Let no man leave of it till the morning.

"Notwithstanding they hearkened not unto Moses; but some of them left of it until the morning, and it bred worms, and stank: and Moses was angry with them.

"And they gathered it every morning, every man according to his eating: and when the sun waxed hot, it melted.

"And it came to pass, that on the sixth day they gathered twice as much bread, two omers for one man: and all the rulers of the congregation came and told Moses" (Ex. 16:19-22).

The command was emphatic. They must not think they could gather a great deal of manna, and that it would do for several days. The Lord told them specifically that they were to gather the manna each morning, with the exception of the Sabbath. If, in fact, they tried to leave it till the next morning in order for it to be used the next day, it would *"breed worms and stink."*

Now, what spiritual meaning does this have?

As we have stated, the manna was a type of Christ. Basically, this is what Christ was referring to when He said, *"If any man will come after Me, let him deny himself, and take up his Cross daily, and follow Me"* (Lk. 9:23).

"Denying oneself," as used here by Christ, is not speaking of asceticism, which refers to the denial of all things that are pleasurable, etc. It is rather speaking of the believer not trusting in himself, but rather trusting totally in Christ.

EVERYTHING COMES BY THE CROSS

When Jesus spoke of taking up the Cross, he said that it must be done *daily,* which, in essence, refers back to the manna.

This simply means that we are to understand that everything we have from the Lord is made possible to us by what Jesus did at the Cross. As well, we must renew our faith daily, so to speak, in the Cross, not depending on that which we had yesterday, etc.

The manna as a type of Christ and the gathering of it each day was meant to proclaim the fact that we must feed upon

Christ each and every day. We must not try to live on yester-day's faith. All of this has to do with our spiritual growth, and if not adhered to as Christ commanded, will result in spiritual declension.

On the sixth day, which would be Friday, they were to gather twice as much manna, which they were not allowed to do on all the other days, with the extra manna being preserved for the Sabbath. On that particular day, it would not breed worms and stink. So, we see here that God was performing all types of miracles as it regarded this wonderful supply.

THE SABBATH

"And he said unto them, This is that which the LORD *has said, Tomorrow is the rest of the Holy Sabbath unto the* LORD*: bake that which you will bake today, and seethe that you will seethe; and that which remains over lay up for you to be kept until the morning"* (Ex. 16:23).

The Sabbath, which is the seventh day and is a Saturday, is now introduced after a lapse of about 2,500 years (Gen. 2:1-3). It was to be a day of rest, which means that no work was to be done on this day.

This rest typified Christ and the spiritual rest that He would bring as it regarded what He would do at the Cross. Salvation can be explained as a *"rest in Christ."* Unfortunately, with millions trying to earn their salvation in one way or the other, we seem not to have learned this lesson very well (Mat. 11:28-30).

This ordinance of the Sabbath was given to Israel only and was not meant to be carried over into the church. In fact, the sacrifices, circumcision, and a host of other things were given to Israel only, and were not carried over into the church because Christ had totally fulfilled all of these types and shadows.

All of this was a type of Christ and what He would do for the human race, at least for those who would believe Him (Jn. 3:16). When He came, He fulfilled all of these types in every capacity.

The manna was not given by the Lord on the Sabbath simply because to have done so would have violated the type. However, He made provision for Israel, as stated, by giving twice as much on the sixth day, which means they were to gather twice as much, but on this day only.

UNBELIEF

"And they laid it up till the morning, as Moses bade: and it did not stink, neither was there any worm therein.

"And Moses said, Eat that today; for today is a Sabbath unto the LORD: today you shall not find it in the field.

"Six days you shall gather it; but on the seventh day, which is the Sabbath, in it there shall be none.

"And it came to pass, that there went out some of the people on the seventh day for to gather, and they found none.

"And the LORD said unto Moses, How long refuse you to keep My commandments and My laws?

"See, for that the LORD *has given you the Sabbath, therefore He gives you on the sixth day the bread of two days; abide you every man in his place, let no man go out of his place on the seventh day.*

"So the people rested on the seventh day" (Ex. 16:24-30).

Despite the commands given, it seems that some persuaded themselves that they knew better. Consequently, they went out on the seventh day to gather manna but *"found none."* From the terminology given in Verse 28, it seems that the Lord was somewhat put out with this refusal to obey Him.

THROUGH CHRIST AND WHAT HE HAS DONE FOR US AT THE CROSS

This is a perfect example of the following problem and, in effect, the greatest problem, I think, in the modern church, and always has been:

Our victory as a child of God comes to us exclusively by and through Christ and what He has done for us at the Cross. We obtain all of these benefits by simply believing in Him and, thereby, trusting in what He did for us in His great sacrifice of Himself. That's the reason I keep explaining the Cross over and over. If the believer doesn't understand it, he will not enter into God's rest, but will instead attempt to earn his salvation in one way or the other.

The Lord had told Israel that on the Sabbath day, they were to do nothing but *rest*. As stated, this typified Christ and what He would do with the human race, and by that, we speak of the Cross. This means that it's not something I do, but rather trusting in something that He has already done. The sad fact is, much of the modern church understands the Cross, at least somewhat, as it refers to salvation, but understands the Cross not at all as it refers to sanctification, in other words, how we live for God and how we order our behavior.

SANCTIFICATION

Unfortunately, one of the single most important principles in the Bible, the principle of sanctification, is all but presently ignored. In fact, most Christians don't have the slightest idea what sanctification actually is.

In the Greek, as a noun, the word is *hagiasmos* and means *"separation to God"* (I Cor. 1:30; II Thess. 2:13; I Pet. 1:2).

Sanctification is a relationship with God into which men enter by faith in Christ (Acts 26:18; I Cor. 6:11), and to which our sole title is the death of Christ, i.e., *"the death of Christ on the Cross"* (Eph. 5:25-26; Col. 1:22; Heb. 10:10, 29; 13:12).

Sanctification is also used in the New Testament of the separation of the believer from evil things and ways. This sanctification is God's will for the believer (I Thess. 4:3) and His purpose in calling us by the gospel as the Holy Spirit teaches it by God's Word (Jn. 17:17, 19; Ps. 17:4; 119:9).

Sanctification is not vicarious, meaning that it cannot be transferred or imputed. It is an individual possession, built up, little by little, as the result of obedience to the Word of God and of following the example of Christ, with our faith ever in the finished work of Christ (Mat. 11:29; Jn. 13:15; Eph. 4:20; Phil. 2:5).

The Holy Spirit is the agent in sanctification (Rom. 15:16; II Thess. 2:13; I Pet. 1:2; I Cor. 6:11). However, the believer must know and understand how the Holy Spirit functions in order for the sanctification process to take its rightful course.

THE LAW OF THE SPIRIT OF LIFE IN CHRIST JESUS

In brief, Paul tells us how the Spirit works in the following Scripture: *"For the law* (the manner in which the Spirit works) *of the Spirit* (Holy Spirit) *of life* (the benefits of the Cross) *in Christ Jesus* (the law of which is spoken here pertains to what Jesus did at the Cross, with the phrase 'in Christ Jesus' always referring to the sacrifice of Christ) *has made me free from the law of sin and death"* (Rom. 8:2).

The believer certainly must be ardently willing for the fruit of the Spirit to be developed in his life, but, other than faith, that is all that is required of the believer. In other words, the believer cannot sanctify himself by doing spiritual things. As stated, we are sanctified solely by the Holy Spirit.

The one thing that is required of us, and that which is so very, very important, is this: The believer must evidence faith in Christ and His great sacrifice. He must understand that not only does salvation come to him through what Jesus did at the Cross, but sanctification as well. The foundation of this is given in Romans 6:3-14.

THE HOLY SPIRIT

When the believer evidences faith in Christ and the Cross, the Holy Spirit — who works within the legal boundaries of the Cross — will then function mightily in the heart and life of such a believer, thereby, developing the fruit of the Spirit and ever drawing the believer closer to God. This is the only manner in which the *"law of sin and death"* can be defeated. In fact, that negative law is so strong that it is only *"the law of the Spirit of life in Christ Jesus"* that can overcome these evil passions.

This is actually what the Sabbath represented — rest in Christ! As stated, the believer cannot sanctify himself, but the Holy Spirit definitely can and will; however, He will do so only as we evidence faith in Christ and His finished work. As long as we make the Cross the object of our faith, the Holy Spirit will then perform His work. If our faith is shifted to other things, irrespective as to what those other things might be, the end result will be *"spiritual adultery"* (Rom. 7:1-4).

The Lord has one manner of sanctification exactly as He has one manner of salvation. It is both, or one should say, all in Christ, and as Paul said, *"Christ and Him crucified"* (I Cor. 1:23).

MANNA

"And the house of Israel called the name thereof manna: and it was like coriander seed, white; and the taste of it was like wafers made with honey" (Ex. 16:31).

Verse 31 proclaims once again the name of the miracle bread from heaven — manna. In the Hebrew, it means,
"What is it?" They had no name for it because there had
never been anything like it on earth previously.

Actually, it was angels' food and was sent from heaven
(Ps. 78:25). As the people would reject the manna, likewise,
they would reject Christ.

The Lord would supply this manna for some 40 years — all
the time the children of Israel wandered in the wilderness — until they came to the land of Canaan.

The manna was a provision made for God's people. It
was not a question of redemption, that having been obtained
in the blood of the Cross, and there alone. The manna was
meant to proclaim Christ and His sustenance for the saints,
and that on a daily basis. The wilderness afforded not one
blade of grass or one drop of water for the Israel of God. In
Jehovah alone was their portion.

It is the same with believers presently. This world is not
our home! Truly, *"here have we no continuing city, but we
seek one to come"* (Heb. 13:14).

CHRIST FOREVER

No wonder Paul wrote that we now have a much better
covenant based on better promises (Heb. 8:6). Whereas
Israel had only the type of Christ, the manna, we now feed
upon a risen and glorified Christ, ascended up to heaven in
virtue of accomplished redemption. This was carried out at

the Cross, and done so by the shedding of His own precious blood (Eph. 2:13-18).

As the manna came every day, with the exception of the Sabbath, this portrays the fact that it was Christ yesterday, and it must be Christ today, and Christ forever. Moreover, it will not do to feed partly on Christ and partly on other things. As in the matter of life, it is Christ alone. So, in the matter of living, it must be Christ alone. As we cannot mingle anything with that which *imparts* life, and I speak of the Cross, so neither can we mingle anything with that which *sustains* it, and I continue to speak of the Cross.

MEMORIAL

"And Moses said, This is the thing which the Lord *commands, Fill an omer of it to be kept for your generations; that they may see the bread wherewith I have fed you in the wilderness, when I brought you forth from the land of Egypt"* (Ex. 16:32).

A container of manna was to be kept as a most precious memorial of the faithfulness of God. Once again, the Lord would perform a miracle.

Whereas the manna held over would normally breed worms and stink, the manna addressed here in this verse could be sustained by the power of God for many, many centuries.

The manna was to ever be a testimony that God did not suffer them to die of hunger, as their foolish hearts had unbelievingly anticipated. He rained bread from heaven on them, fed them with angels' food, watched over them with all the tenderness of a nurse, did bear with them, and carried them on eagles' wings, so to speak. Had they only continued on the proper ground of faith, He would have put them in eternal possession of all the promises made to their fathers.

IF GOD HAS DONE IT ...

While we do not live off of past blessings, at the same time, we are to never forget the past blessings, allowing them to be proof positive of what God can do and, in fact, has done.

This we must remember: If God has done it in the past, He will definitely do it in the present and in the future. If He has ever opened a blinded eye, unstopped a deaf ear, or unloosed a captive tongue, He most definitely will do it again. If He has ever set a captive free and loosed him from the chains that bound him, He will do it again! If He has ever answered prayer, opened the windows of heaven, or granted us that which He alone can grant, He will do it again! If He has ever baptized one believer with the Holy Spirit, and has done so with the evidence of speaking with other tongues, He will do it again! And if He came once, He most definitely will come again!

Furthermore, God never regresses but ever goes forward, and as He goes forward, He always, and without exception, enlarges the revelation. So, what He did yesterday, He will do today, but He will do it even on a greater scale, that is, if God's people will only believe Him.

That's why Jesus wondrously said, *"Verily, verily, I say unto you, He who believes on Me, the works that I do shall he do also; and greater works than these shall he do; because I go unto My Father"* (Jn. 14:12).

GREATER WORKS?

How in the world could believers presently do greater works than Christ? And yet, this is exactly what He said would happen. He was speaking of the expanding revelation. Men could only say that He would do this, but after the Cross, we can now say, "He has done it." To be sure, the possession is always greater than the promise!

THE POT OF MANNA

"And Moses said unto Aaron, Take a pot, and put an omer full of manna therein, and lay it up before the LORD, to be kept for your generations.

"As the LORD commanded Moses, so Aaron laid it up before the Testimony, to be kept" (Ex. 16:33-34).

The omer was a man's daily portion. Laid up before the Lord, it furnished a volume of truth. There was no worm therein or ought of taint. It was the record of Jehovah's faithfulness in providing for those whom He had redeemed out of the hand of the enemy.

As stated, this was not so when man hoarded it up for himself. Then the symptoms of corruption soon made their appearance. If entering into the truth and reality of our position in Christ, we cannot hoard up. It is our privilege, day by day, to enter into the preciousness of Christ as the One who came down from heaven to give life unto the world.

THE TESTIMONY

However, if any try to live off of past experiences, thereby, failing to renew Christ afresh in their hearts daily, one will find spiritual declension setting in as is regards their experiences, and in the words of Scripture, *"breeding worms and stinking."*

The *"pot of manna"* was laid up before the Lord, with the *"tables of the covenant"* and *"Aaron's rod that budded."*

The *"testimony"* was the Law of Moses, and more specifically, the moral law, i.e., *"the Ten Commandments"* (Ex., Chpt. 20). The law presents the righteousness of God and that which He demands of man.

As repeatedly stated, the *"pot of manna"* represented Christ, who alone *"kept the testimony,"* and did it on our behalf, even as the last Adam (I Cor. 15:45-50).

"Aaron's rod that budded," proclaims the life that comes exclusively from our High Priest, the Lord Jesus Christ, and our faith in Him, who paid the price for our redemption on the Cross of Calvary. As stated, it is all of Christ, in Christ, about Christ, with Christ, and alone Christ!

FORTY YEARS

"And the children of Israel did eat manna forty years, until they came to a land inhabited; they did eat manna, until they came unto the borders of the land of Canaan.

"Now an omer is the tenth part of an ephah" (Ex. 16:35-36).

As the Lord continued the provision for the children of Israel until they came *"unto the borders of the land of Canaan,"* He does the same with believers presently.

The wilderness was not exactly a place of victory for the children of Israel. In fact, all of that generation died in the wilderness, with the exception of the children (all 19 and under) and Joshua and Caleb. Those who died, died because of unbelief, but yet, the manna continued. It is the same with believers presently.

When the new generation came to *"the borders of the land of Canaan,"* the manna ceased, and they were instructed by the Lord to eat the *"old corn of the land."*

The Scripture then said, *"And the manna ceased on the morrow after they had eaten of the old corn of the land; neither had the children of Israel manna anymore; but they did eat of the fruit of the land of Canaan that year"* (Josh. 5:11-12).

NOW WHAT DOES THAT TELL US?

As new believers, the Lord will bear with us, even for a long while. He will continue giving the manna, that is, making Himself real to us, irrespective of our stumblings, etc. However, there will come a time when He will demand that we grow up. And how do we do that?

The believer should be taught from the moment of conversion that his spiritual growth consists totally and completely in Christ and what Christ did at the Cross on his behalf. The Cross of Christ must ever be the object of one's faith.

While it is true that the Holy Spirit is the One who performs the task in our lives, which, in fact, is unending, and I speak of spiritual growth, still, He carries out His great work solely on the premise of the sacrifice of Christ (Rom. 8:2).

Paul said: *"But if the Spirit* (Holy Spirit) *of Him* (God the Father) *who raised up Jesus from the dead dwell in you, He* (God the Father) *who raised up Christ from the dead shall also quicken your mortal bodies by His Spirit who dwells in you"* (Rom. 8:11).

The *"quickening of our mortal bodies"* doesn't pertain to the coming resurrection, but rather to our everyday living for God. After awhile, the manna will stop, and you will now be expected to eat the *"old corn of the land,"* i.e., *"abide strictly by the Word."*

> *Where He may lead me I will go,*
> *For I have learned to trust Him so,*
> *And I remember 'twas for me,*
> *That He was slain on Calvary."*

O I delight in His command,
Love to be led by His dear hand;
His divine will is sweet to me,
Hallowed by His blood-stained Calvary.

Onward I go, no doubt, no fear,
Happy with Christ my Saviour near,
Trusting that I someday shall see
Jesus my friend of Calvary.

THE WORLD THE FLESH AND THE DEVIL

CHAPTER 3

THE SMITTEN ROCK

THE SMITTEN ROCK

"AND ALL THE CONGREGATION of the children of Israel journeyed from the wilderness of Sin, after their journeys, according to the commandment of the LORD, and pitched in Rephidim: and there was no water for the people to drink" (Ex. 17:1).

Once again, faith must be tested. They are taken by the *"commandment of the Lord"* to *"Rephidim."*

It would seem somewhat strange that God, who professed to love Israel, should lead them into a desert without food and water; however, it was love that led them there that they might learn the desperate unbelief of their own hearts.

The child of God does not really know what he is until tested, and neither can the child of God know who God is until tested. In this situation, Israel would have nothing without God, but with God, they would have everything.

As we shall see, Verses 5 through 7 record one of the greatest miracles, plus one of the greatest *"types,"* found in the entire Word of God.

The phrase, *"The commandment of the* LORD," means that their journey was being led by the Lord. In other words, the cloud moved, giving them direction.

As we stated, it was love that led them to this waterless place. In fact, every single thing that the Lord does for us or to us as His children is motivated 100 percent by love.

Everything the Lord leads us into is always done for our good. Here they would learn the desperate unbelief of their own hearts and the unfailing faithfulness of God's heart. Only in a desert could God reveal what He can be to those who trust Him, for only there was Israel dependent upon Him for everything. Without God, they had nothing; with God, they had everything.

Rephidim means *"resting place."* This was an oasis, but at certain times of the year, the copious stream dries up, and evidently, this was one of those times.

THE PATH OF FAITH

How so much all of this illustrates the fact that the path of faith is a path of trial. Those who are led by God must expect to encounter that which is displeasing to the flesh and also a constant and real testing of faith itself. God's design is to wean us from everything down here, to bring us to the place where we have no reliance upon material and human resources, and to cast us completely upon Him.

Oh, how slow, how painfully slow we are to learn this lesson! How miserably and how repeatedly we fail! How longsuffering the Lord is with us! It is to this that the introductory *"and"* is designed to point.

The Scripture says, *"There was no water for the people to drink."*

Did they remember that a few days before God had sweetened the bitter waters of Marah? Did they remember that God had opened a path through the Red Sea?

In fact, the Lord certainly knew there was no water there, and yet, He directed them to this very place. As we will see momentarily, their reaction was again to *"murmur and complain."*

HOW DOES IT FIT US PERSONALLY?

Before we criticize Israel too strongly and, thereby, be quick to point out their faults and failures, I think we ought to take a look at ourselves. Are we doing any better? Do we rejoice when the blessings come and find fault and complain when the tests and the trials come our way?

You see, anybody can praise God when the windows of heaven are open; however, when those windows close, it's not easy to praise God then.

Let us say it again: Every single thing that happens to us is designed by the Lord. We're not our own; we are bought with a price. That price is the shed blood of the Lord Jesus Christ. As well, the Lord is training us for something. We must realize that He is not only the One who leads us into blessing, which He definitely does, but, as well, He is the One who leads us to the place of testing. He is the same God on both counts. As we have also stated, it is love that leads us to both places, and it is to show us our needs.

As we said some pages back, we learn a lot about God during the times of blessings, but we don't learn very much about ourselves. We can only learn about ourselves during times of testing.

MURMURING

"Wherefore the people did chide with Moses, and said, Give us water that we may drink. And Moses said unto them, Why chide you with me? wherefore do you tempt the LORD?

"And the people thirsted there for water; and the people murmured against Moses, and said, Wherefore is this that you have brought us up out of Egypt, to kill us and our children and our cattle with thirst?" (Ex. 17:2-3).

The questions of the wilderness are:

What?

Where?

How?

Faith has a brief but comprehensive answer to all three, namely, *God!*

There are several things here that must be noted:

First of all, we see that the people complained to Moses in a form of astute criticism, but let the reader understand that when we criticize God's man, we are, in essence, criticizing God. Hence, Moses would ask, *"Wherefore do you tempt the LORD?"*

To tempt the Lord is to exhibit a want of faith, which arouses His anger and provokes Him. It was the special sin of the Israelites during the whole period of their sojourn in the wilderness. They *"tempted and provoked the Most High God"* (Ps. 78:56). They *"provoked Him to anger with their inventions"* (Ps. 106:29). They *"provoked Him at the sea"* (Ps. 106:7). They *"tempted God in the desert"* (Ps. 106:14). Considering all of this, God's longsuffering can only be looked at as amazing.

THIRST

Next, we find the people *murmuring*, and doing so against Moses, which, as stated, is the same as murmuring against God. And yet, the Lord would take Israel to a higher height of spiritual revelation than they had yet seen. However, let it be understood that He does this despite their murmuring and complaining — which we shall momentarily see — and certainly not because of it. As we've just quoted from Psalms, the Holy Spirit noted all the murmurings and complaining and recorded it for posterity. So, this tells us how displeased the Lord was with the actions of the children of Israel.

At the same time, the phrase, *"the people thirsted there for water,"* signifies intense thirst.

It is said that there is probably no physical affliction comparable to intense thirst. His thirst was the only agony that drew from the Son of Man an acknowledgment of physical suffering, and did so in the words *"I thirst."*

So, their thirst was real, very real! Of course, the Lord knew this and, as well, knew exactly what He was going to do.

THE TEST!

Unfortunately, in the last few decades, a great part of the modern church — in its embracing of the Word of Faith doctrine — has tried to eliminate all testing, etc. They teach that a proper confession will rid one of such activity. Why would one need testing when one is already perfectly righteous and, in fact, a little god?

However, erroneous teaching regarding this subject, or even denying the validity of testing, in no way exempts the believer, that is, the true believer, from God's way. To be sure, His way is the way of testing, which He does constantly.

Considering the fact that a great percentage of people adhering to this doctrine are not really even born again, there is no testing, of course, for such individuals. They don't belong to the Lord and, in fact, have nothing to test. However, considering those who are truly born again, the testing will come, irrespective of what they have been taught. As someone has well said, faith must always be tested, and great faith must be tested greatly.

BEWILDERED AND CONFUSED

The problem is, for such individuals who have believed that which is error, and I continue to speak of the Word of

Faith doctrine, testing leaves them bewildered and confused because it's against everything that they have been taught. Although truly born again, many at this stage simply lose faith. They have been taught that none of these things will happen if they have the proper confession, but Jesus said that irrespective of what we have been taught, *"The rain descended, and the floods came, and the winds blew, and beat upon that house."* If the house is built upon the rock of true faith, and we speak of faith in Christ and what He has done for us at the Cross, it will not fall because it is *"founded upon a rock."* But otherwise, it will fall *and great will be the fall of it* (Mat. 7:25-27).

The idea is not whether the rain and the floods will come, and the winds will blow; that is a given. The idea is, do you have proper faith?

PROPER FAITH

What is proper faith?

It is obvious that the children of Israel had their faith placed in other things. Their faith should have been in the slain lamb, inasmuch as they surely realized that this is what caused Pharaoh to buckle. Instead, their faith was in something else, whether themselves or whatever; it made no difference. Unless it's faith in Christ and Him crucified, then it's not faith that God will honor. Now, let the reader read these words very carefully.

The sadness is, for the last several decades, the Word of Faith doctrine has talked about faith as it has talked about nothing else, but with the truth being that there is less true faith in the church presently than ever before in its history. Yes, it is faith, but not the kind that God will recognize.

Paul held up faith as no other apostle, and rightly so. He understood faith as no one else in the world of his day. For it to be true faith, the type of faith that God will always recognize, it had to be faith in Christ and the Cross. That's why he said: *"For in Jesus Christ neither circumcision avails anything, nor uncircumcision; but faith which works by love"* (Gal. 5:6).

John said: *"This is the victory that overcomes the world, even our faith"* (I Jn. 5:4).

When false teachers came into the churches in Galatia and were teaching *"another gospel,"* which would pull them away from true faith, Paul said very testily: *"But though we, or an angel from heaven, preach any other gospel unto you than that which we have preached unto you, let him be accursed"* (Gal. 1:8).

The Cross of Christ must ever be the object of our faith. When it is the object of our faith, we will begin to see the Bible in an entirely different light and actually understand it to a far greater degree than ever before. In fact, the story of the Bible is the story of the Cross.

MOSES

"And Moses cried unto the LORD, saying, What shall I do unto this people? they be almost ready to stone me" (Ex. 17:4).

Concerning this moment, Pulpit Commentary says: "It is one of the most prominent traits of the character of Moses, that at the occurrence of a difficulty, he always carries it straight to God" (Ex. 15:25; 24:15; 32:30; 33:8; Num. 11:2, 11; 12:11; 14:13-19).

The fact that we are told that Moses *"cried unto the* LORD*"* indicates the earnestness and vehemence of his prayer. *"What shall I do?"* expressed a consciousness of his own inability to cope with the situation, and also showed his confidence that the Lord would come to his and their relief.

When facing problems and difficulties that we cannot solve — in fact, even if we think we can solve them — every believer should always go to the Lord, whether the situation is large or small, and say, *"What shall I do?"* Down through life, I have learned that the Holy Spirit, who is God, is an architect, a builder, a plumber, a truck driver, a pilot, a teacher, a fund-raiser, and, in fact, anything that we need.

As believers, let us never think that it is men who do the doing. While God might use men, and often does, it is still the Lord who has maneuvered events, places, things, and people. We should look to Him for everything.

LOOK TO GOD

I get amused at times regarding some young people who are considering our Bible college. Some will ask the question, "After I graduate, who will get me a church?" implying that denominational heads can provide such, and we can't. They are missing the point altogether. The very question says that their faith is in man and not God. As such, irrespective as to where they go, they will serve no purpose for the Lord. In fact, they are a waste of time, that is, if they stay in that frame of mind.

To be sure, if they come to this school, they will be taught to look to the Lord for leading, guidance, and, in fact, for everything. Even if man wants to help, he can only work within the limitation of man. God has no limitations and can do all things. So, it would make much better sense to look to God.

Moses cried unto the Lord, and we must do the same. We must not grow weary in doing this, and above all, we must not be faithless. If the answer doesn't come immediately, we are to continue. Our Lord said as much: *"I say unto you, Though he will not rise and give him, because he is his friend, yet because of his importunity* (overly persistent in demand or request) *he will rise and give him as many as he needs.*

"And I say unto you, Ask, and it shall be given you; seek, and you shall find; knock, and it shall be opened unto you." The Lord then promised this:

"For every one who asks receives; and he who seeks finds; and to him who knocks it shall be opened."

And then: *"If a son shall ask bread of any of you who is a father, will he give him a stone? or if he ask a fish, will he for a fish give him a serpent?*

"Or if he shall ask an egg, will he offer him a scorpion (an egg containing a scorpion)?*"*

And finally: *"If you then, being evil, know how to give good gifts unto your children: how much more shall your heavenly Father give the Holy Spirit (who makes possible all of these things) to them who ask Him?"* (Lk. 11:8-13)

PRAYER

Why is it that prayer is almost a lost art in the modern church? Why is it that most Christians, in fact, almost none, take advantage of the great privilege to take our needs to our heavenly Father? There are several reasons.

First of all, there is a higher percentage presently of unre-deemed people in the church than there has been in the last 200 to 300 years. Even in churches that claim to be funda-mental, which means they claim to believe all of the Bible, I think I can say without fear of exaggeration that most of the people in these churches aren't born again. A percentage is, but I fear that percentage is small.

Secondly, even among those who are truly born again, unbelief regarding prayer is rampant, which is obvious because we see so few Christians who have any prayer life at all. However, it's the type of unbelief that is enmeshed in false doctrine, not so much a rank disavowal of the Word of God.

THE WORD OF FAITH DOCTRINE

The reason for this unbelief regarding prayer, I think, can be laid at the doorstep of the Word of Faith doctrine, which, in reality, is no faith at all. In fact, this doctrine teaches that if a person seeks the Lord on a regular basis, this shows that something is wrong, and there can be nothing wrong, they say, with a new creation man, etc. They do not teach their adherents to seek the Lord, but rather to *"confess"* their way to riches, etc. So, prayer is out, and confession is in. As stated, this has had a greater effect on the church than any other false doctrine, or even a culmination of false doctrines.

As well, the Word of Faith doctrine pulls believers from the Cross and actually repudiates the Cross. They claim that the Cross is little more than *past miseries.* It is referred to by their chief teachers as *the greatest defeat in human history.* They claim that if the preacher preaches the Cross, he is preaching death, etc. That is strange, especially considering that Paul said: *"For the preaching of the Cross is to them who perish foolishness; but unto us who are saved it is the power of God"* (I Cor. 1:18).

A PROPER UNDERSTANDING OF THE CROSS

I think, as well, that a proper understanding of the Cross, with one's faith anchored firmly in that finished work and refusal to allow it to be moved, is the criterion for both understanding the Word of God and having a successful, consistent prayer life. Israel's safety, protection, leading, guidance, prosperity, and, in fact, everything she received from the Lord, was predicated solely on the slain lamb. The sacrificial system, which symbolized the coming Christ and what He would do to redeem humanity — which refers to going to the Cross — presented itself as the very center of the Old Testament economy. As well, the Cross of Christ functions in the same manner for the New Testament economy, except that now, this is a work that's already done instead of that which is to be done in the future, making it much easier to understand and receive.

To fail to understand the Cross is in some way to fail to understand the entirety of the Word of God. In other words, the Cross is the key to the Word, while faith is the key to the Cross (Rom. 6:3-14; Gal. 2:20; 5:6; Eph. 2:13-18; Col. 2:10-15).

GOD'S PRESCRIBED ORDER OF LIFE AND LIVING

- Jesus Christ is the source of all things we receive from God (Jn. 1:1-3, 14, 29; Rom. 6:1-14).
- The Cross of Christ is the means, and the only means, by which all these wonderful things are given to us (I Cor. 1:17-18, 21, 23; 2:2).
- What Jesus did at the Cross must be the object of our faith at all times, with us understanding that it's the Cross that is the means (Col. 2:10-15).
- Understanding that Jesus is the source, the Cross is the means, and the Cross of Christ must be the object of our faith, the Holy Spirit will then work mightily on our behalf as only He can do. He doesn't require much of us, but He does require, actually insists, that our faith be properly placed in Christ and the Cross (Rom. 8:1-11; Eph. 2:13-18).

THE ROD

*"And the LORD said unto Moses, Go on before the peo-
ple, and take with you of the elders of Israel; and your rod,
wherewith you smote the river, take in your hand, and go"*
(Ex. 17:5).

By the elders of Israel going with Moses, it made them
a witness of what was to transpire, and, as well, they served
as representatives of the people. In effect, this made them a
part of the miracle that was to transpire. By doing this, the
Lord was informing Israel that each and every person must
call upon the Lord. In other words, quit murmuring and start
praying and praising. We serve a miracle-working God. If it's
food we need, He will give food! If it's water we need, He will
give water! If it's money we need, He will give money! If it's
victory we need, He will give victory

While Moses under God was definitely their leader, and
they were always to look to him as such, the idea is, every single individual in Israel, be it man, woman, boy, or girl, was
to be a person of faith. I quite often tell our church (Family Worship Center) that I want them to be people of faith. I
want them to believe in what we are doing, in what God has
called us to do.

A PART OF THE VISION

The Lord guided and directed Israel through prophets.
He guides and directs the church through apostles. Empha-

sis and direction are given to apostles, which is borne out in the book of Acts and the epistles. The Lord gives revelation to apostles, whomever they might be, which, incidentally, will always coincide perfectly with the Word. As He gives this revelation, he also calls a great number of people to support that apostle and stand with him. Even though this that the Lord gives him affects the entirety of the body of Christ all over the world, the Lord will always make certain that enough helping hands are given to ensure the propagation of the revelation or vision. So, in essence, these particular people, whomever they are privileged to be, actually become a part of the revelation. It's almost like the Lord is giving them the revelation, as well, which, in a sense, He is.

THE REVELATION OF THE CROSS

In 1997, the Lord began to give me the revelation of the Cross, which has gloriously changed my life. As I continue to say, it's not anything new, actually that which was given to the Apostle Paul, and he gave to us in his 14 epistles. However, the church has had so little preaching and teaching on the Cross in the last several decades that, by and large, it is presently illiterate as it regards this very foundation of the gospel. Consequently, the modern church little knows where it has been, where it is, or where it is going. So, this vision of the Cross, as should be overly obvious, is vitally significant.

In 2010, the Lord began to give me a vision of the way and manner in which this great revelation of the Cross can be taken to the world. He told us to begin a television network, airing this message 24 hours a day, seven days a week. He also said that we were not to sell time to other preachers, but that all ministry must come out of Family Worship Center. In other words, He wanted the message to be the same from all the preachers, whomever they might be. That message is to be *Jesus Christ and Him crucified*.

Considering the way the Lord said to do such a ministry, when we began, most said it was impossible to succeed, but, miracle of miracles, it did succeed. At the time of this writing, we are now in 72 million homes in the U.S., 24 hours a day, seven days a week, and actually, we are adding more homes constantly. He also told us to go through every door that He would open in other countries of the world. That's exactly what we are doing, and we are now airing in nearly a hundred countries of the world. It is the message that propels this network, the Message of the Cross. Some 2,000 years ago, the early church began with the Message of the Cross, and it is going out with the Message of the Cross, meaning that it will have come full circle.

A PART OF THE VISION

All who believe in what we are doing and, thereby, support what we are doing, both prayerfully and financially, literally become a part of the vision. In a sense, as stated, God is giving them the revelation as He has given it to me.

In fact, all of the people of Israel, in a sense, were to conduct themselves exactly as Moses. Regrettably, they didn't, and regrettably, that generation perished in the wilderness.

The rod, of which Verse 5 speaks, was a symbol of judgment. The first reference to it definitely determines that. When Moses, in front of Pharaoh, placed it on the floor, it became a serpent (Ex. 4:3) — a reminder of the curse. With this rod, the waters of the Nile were smitten and turned into blood (Ex. 7:17). This proclaims the fact that the only answer to this curse is the shed blood of the Lord Jesus Christ. So, now, the rod would smite the rock — symbolic of Christ being smitten by God on the Cross — from which would come the life-giving rivers of water. I remind the reader that it wasn't the resurrection, as wonderful and as necessary as that was, which produced this, but rather the Cross.

THE ROCK

"Behold, I will stand before you there upon the rock in Horeb; and you shall smite the rock, and there shall come water out of it, that the people may drink. And Moses did so in the sight of the elders of Israel" (Ex. 17:6).

We are now about to witness one of the many Old Testament types of the Lord Jesus, in fact, one of the most graphic of all. Concerning this type, Paul said:

"Moreover, brethren, I would not that you should be ignorant, how that all our fathers were under the cloud (the cloud of the presence of the Lord, which led Israel in the wil-

derness), *and all passed through the sea* (the great Red Sea miracle); *and were all baptized under Moses in the cloud and in the sea* (meaning that it was Moses whom God used to bring about these miracles, which were 'types'); *and did all eat the same spiritual meat; and did all drink the same spiritual drink: for they drank of that spiritual rock that followed them: and that rock was Christ"* (I Cor. 10:1-4).

THE ROCK WAS TO BE SMITTEN

In fact, Christ personally affirmed that by saying *"upon this rock* (pointing to Himself and not referring to Peter's confession) *I will build My church"* (Mat. 16:18).

This *rock* was to be smitten. This, of course, speaks of the death of the Lord Jesus. It is striking to note the *order* of the teaching as it regards the *types* given in Exodus, Chapters 16 and 17. In the former, we have that which speaks of the incarnation of Christ, and we speak of the giving of the manna. In Chapter 17, we see that which foreshadows the crucifixion of Christ, and, of course, we speak of the smitten rock. Christ had to descend from heaven to earth (as the manna did) if He was to become the Bread of Life to His people; but He must be smitten by divine judgment if He was to be the Water of Life to them!

THE TIMING OF THE SMITTEN ROCK

Exodus, Chapter 17, opens not with praise and worship as it should, but rather with murmuring and complaining. This was the occasion of the smitten rock. However, *"where sin abounded, grace did much more abound"* (Rom. 5:20).

Jesus did not die on the Cross because the people were righteous and holy, but rather because they were the very opposite. He died on the Cross because of sin and shame, transgression and iniquity, and because man desperately needed Christ and what Christ would do on the Cross, even though man was actually not aware of his terrible condition.

That's why Jesus said: *"They who be whole need not a physician, but they who are sick.*

"But go you and learn what that means, I will have mercy, and not sacrifice: for I am not come to call the righteous, but sinners to repentance" (Mat. 9:12-13).

WATER OUT OF THE ROCK

The rock mentioned here must have been of gigantic size. The water that would come out of it had to slake the thirst not only for approximately 3 million Israelites but, as well, all of their cattle and sheep.

In fact, the psalmist referred to this. He said:

"He (God) *cleaved the rocks in the wilderness, and gave them drink as out of the great depths.*

"He brought streams also out of the rock, and caused waters to run down like rivers" (Ps. 78:15-16).

The psalmist also said: *"Which turned the rock into a standing water, the flint into a fountain of waters"* (Ps. 114:8).

So, what we're speaking of here was not a mere stream, but rather a river of water, which, of course, was needed.

This is what Jesus was speaking about when He said: *"If any man thirst, let him come unto Me, and drink.*

"He who believes on Me, as the Scripture has said, out of his belly shall flow rivers of living water" (Jn. 7:37-38).

THE HOLY SPIRIT

In essence, this living water represented the *Holy Spirit.* The smiting of the rock by Moses, which symbolized God smiting Christ (instead of us), which refers to the Cross, made it possible for the advent of the Holy Spirit in the hearts and lives of all believers. Before the Cross, the Holy Spirit was very limited as to what He could do regarding believers.

That's why Jesus said: *"Even the Spirit of truth; whom the world cannot receive, because it sees Him not, neither knows Him: but you know Him; for He dwells with you, and shall be in you"* (Jn. 14:17).

The disciples, of course, knew exactly what Christ was talking about. This means that before the Cross, the Holy Spirit could dwell with believers, which He definitely did, but could not abide in them permanently. In truth, He did come into some believers to help them perform certain tasks, but only for a period of time.

After the Cross, which atoned for all sin, Jesus said, *"I will pray the Father, and He shall give you another Comforter* (Helper), *that He may abide with you forever"* (Jn. 14:16).

THE HOLY SPIRIT AND THE GODHEAD

The Holy Spirit is the member of the Godhead through whom everything works on this earth. In other words, whatever is done on this earth by God is done by and through the Holy Spirit. The only thing, in fact, that the Holy Spirit didn't do was that which Christ carried out by coming from Heaven, being born of a virgin, and then going to the Cross to satisfy the terrible sin debt. Even then, the Holy Spirit attended Christ every step of the way and throughout every moment of time (Ps. 45:7; Lk. 4:18-19).

Due to the Cross, which is beautifully symbolized by the smitten rock, the Holy Spirit now has far greater latitude to work than He did before the Cross. Again, let us emphasize that it was the Cross that made all of this possible and not the resurrection of Christ, as important as that was.

WHY WAS THE CROSS SUCH A NECESSITY?

To show the reader how much of a necessity it was, upon death, all of the Old Testament saints were actually taken captive by Satan down into paradise (Eph. 4:8-10). While the Evil One could not put them into the burning side of hell — with a great gulf separating that part from paradise (Lk. 16:26) — still, all the Old Testament saints were his captives.

Why was that the case?

Paul said it very clearly: *"For it is not possible that the blood of bulls and of goats should take away sins"* (Heb. 10:4).

In other words, the sin debt that hung heavily over man could not be assuaged by animal blood. So, in effect, the sin debt remained, which means that Satan, at least after a fashion, still had a claim on these individuals, even the greatest of the ones of the Old Testament.

But when Jesus went to the Cross, as Peter said, we *"were not redeemed with corruptible things, as silver and gold ... But with the precious blood of Christ, as of a lamb without blemish and without spot: who verily was foreordained before the foundation of the world, but was manifest in these last times for you"* (I Pet. 1:18-20).

LED CAPTIVITY CAPTIVE

After the death of Christ, even as we've previously stated in this volume, Christ went down into Paradise and led captivity captive. This means that all of these who had been captives of Satan — and all were — were now captives of the Lord Jesus Christ because Christ is the strongest of the strong. He said, *"How can one enter into a strong man's house, and spoil his goods, except he first bind the strong man? and then he will spoil his house"* (Mat. 12:29).

While Satan was strong, Jesus was and is much stronger, as would be obvious; consequently, He did spoil Satan's house, and there was nothing the Evil One could do about it.

I want to remind the reader that Jesus set these people free before the resurrection because the debt was paid at the Cross. Now, when a believer dies, he immediately goes to be with Christ, for Satan has no claim on him whatsoever (Phil. 1:23).

THE LIVING WATER

When the people drank of that water, it slaked their physical thirst, even as it was meant to do. However, it was a type of the living water afforded by Christ and brought to us by the Holy Spirit, which was paid for at Calvary's Cross. There may be other types in the Old Testament as potent as it regards the Cross of Christ, but I think there is none more potent.

Let the following ever be understood: As Israel then drank to their full, that river, so to speak, is still flowing, and all who come may drink to their fill. The water from the smitten rock foretold the Living Water, the Holy Spirit, to be sent forth by the smitten Saviour. The Holy Spirit was the fruit of Christ's sacrifice (I Cor. 10:4).

As we have stated, the rock was smitten by the very same rod of judgment that smote the land of Egypt.

THE TEMPTING OF THE LORD

"And he called the name of the place Massah, and Meribah, because of the chiding of the children of Israel, and because they tempted the LORD, saying, Is the LORD among us, or not?" (Ex. 17:7).

Massah means "trial or temptation."

Meribah means "chiding or quarrel."

To show how displeased the Lord was with the action of the children of Israel, He did not tell Moses to refer to the great miracle of the smitten rock, but rather to place the names of *temptation* and *quarreling* on the place. What an indictment!

One should notice that the temptation, which refers to the name *Massah*, was the fact that they tempted God.

What does that mean? It means that they tried Him to such an extent, and did so by quarreling, murmuring, and complaining, that He was sorely tried as it regarded eliminating the entirety of this people. This shows us exactly how contemptible in the eyes of God is the act of faithlessness. The Lord can take many things that are negative and bear with them far longer than we could ever think of doing so, but He angers quickly as it regards a lack of faith. Of course, I'm speaking of faith as it regards His children.

The Lord wants us to believe Him, and He wants us to believe Him with praises, with victory, and even with shouts of joy. To be frank, the Psalms are full of examples.

Now, it's easy to do that when all things are going well, but it's something else again when nothing, seemingly, is going well.

GOD DOES NOT CHANGE

However, we must remember this — irrespective of circumstances, difficulties, events, problems, trouble, etc. — God does not change. He's the same when blessing us as when putting us to the test. The idea is that we be brought to the place where we do not change either, irrespective of the circumstances.

We must remember that God cannot fail. Our Word of Faith friends claim that God was the biggest failure ever, with them then listing Adam's circumstances, along with many others. They cap it all off by the crucifixion, calling that "the greatest defeat in human history."

The problem is, they are reading in the middle of the book. If they'll read the last two chapters, they will plainly see that we win, which means that God wins, and does so gloriously. No, God has never been defeated, will never be defeated, and, in fact, cannot be defeated!

We cannot be defeated either if we will hold our heads high and look unto Jesus, the author and finisher of our faith (Heb. 12:2). This Hebrews text plainly tells us that what the Lord starts, He finishes. Let every believer to whom the Devil has lied, telling them that they won't make it, understand that whatever the Lord has begun, the Lord will finish!

Irrespective of circumstances, we must believe Him. That means that in time of trouble and difficulties, our demeanor should be the same because the Lord won't fail us.

THE CROSS

There's one other thing I must say in regard to this: Proper faith is required if one is to be what one ought to be. By proper faith, we're speaking of the correct object of faith, which must always be the Cross of Christ.

I want the reader to understand just how important all of this is. As we've previously stated, Paul used the term *"in Christ,"* or one of its derivatives, some 170 times in his 14 epistles. In fact, these two words, *"in Christ,"* explain biblical Christianity as nothing else.

Without exception, those two words refer to what Jesus did at the Cross and our faith in that finished work (Rom. 6:3-14). Everyone talks about faith, but most of the time, it is misplaced faith. God loves faith, but it has to be faith in the finished work of Christ, which means that we understand that all things come to us exclusively through what Jesus did at the Cross. This is the means and the manner in which the Holy Spirit works, and, of course, anything that enables Him to do His work in a greater way is the greatest thing that could ever happen to us. To be sure, the Cross provides such latitude.

AMALEK

"Then came Amalek, and fought with Israel in Rephidim" (Ex. 17:8).

The reception of the Holy Spirit immediately causes war, and we speak of spiritual warfare.

There is an immense difference between justification and sanctification. The one is Christ fighting for us; the other, the Holy Spirit fighting in us.

The entrance of the new nature is the beginning of warfare with the old. Amalek pictures the old carnal nature. This carnal nature wars against the Spirit. *"It is not subject to the law of God, neither indeed can be"* (Rom. 8:7). God has decreed war against it forever.

God did not destroy Amalek but determined to have war with him from generation to generation. He was to dwell in the land but not to reign in it. Romans 6:12 says, *"Let not sin therefore reign in your mortal body."*

This command would have no meaning if sin, i.e., *"the sin nature,"* were not existing in the Christian. Sin dwells in the believer but dwells and reigns in an unbeliever. Verse 14 is the birth of the Bible as a written book. It is remarkable that the first mention of the Bible should be in connection with the hostility of the natural man (Amalek) to the spiritual man (Israel).

As it regards the Bible, no book has been so hated and so loved.

THE PLAN OF REDEMPTION

Beginning with Chapter 12 of Exodus and concluding with Chapter 17, we have a beautiful description of the plan of redemption and how it functions within our hearts and lives.

It is as follows:

- Chapter 12 proclaims the Passover, which typified the great price paid for our redemption in the death of Christ on the Cross.

- In Exodus, Chapter 14, the Red Sea crossing typified the believer's entrance into Christ, and what His crucifixion means to us.
- Chapter 15 proclaims a great rejoicing of the children of Israel on yonder shore, which typified the joy of salvation that comes to the believing sinner.
- The latter portion of Chapter 15 also proclaims the Cross as the answer for life's problems, typified by the bitter waters of Marah and the tree placed in those waters, which made them sweet.
- Chapter 16 proclaims the manna, which was a type of Christ and His blessings to the believer.
- Chapter 16 also proclaims the Sabbath, which is a type of the rest that one experiences after coming to Christ.
- The smitten rock of Chapter 17 portrays the crucifixion of Christ and the living water that flowed from that rock, which typified the Holy Spirit, all made possible by the Cross.
- Last of all, as previously stated, upon the reception of the Holy Spirit, the latter portion of Chapter 17 proclaims the coming of Amalek, a type of the flesh. Satan little opposes the believer who is not Spirit-filled. However, once the believer is baptized with the Holy Spirit — which we teach is always accompanied by the speaking with other tongues (Acts 2:4) — Satan knows that such a believer can cause him much trouble. So, now we have the struggle between the flesh and the Spirit.

WHAT DO WE MEAN BY FLESH?

Paul used the term *"the flesh"* more than anyone else. It is extremely important to note that his use of the term was far more prominent in Chapter 8 of Romans and throughout the entirety of the epistle to the Galatians.

The flesh is that which is indicative of a human being, in other words, our education, motivation, personal talent, personal ability, will power, etc. It's what a human being can do. Within itself, these things aren't necessarily wrong, but we have to quickly come to the knowledge that even though we live in the flesh, we do not war after the flesh. In other words, we cannot live for God by means of the flesh. It simply cannot be done. But yet, not understanding the Cross of Christ as it refers to our sanctification and how the Holy Spirit works, the sad truth is, virtually the entirety of the church world — and I speak of those who truly love the Lord — are trying to live for God by means of the flesh.

Romans, Chapter 8, is the Holy Spirit chapter, one might say. As someone has said, Romans, Chapter 6, portrays to us the *mechanics* of the Holy Spirit. In other words, it tells us *how* He does things, or more particularly, the manner in which He does them, which is by the Cross. Romans, Chapter 8, proclaims to us the *dynamics* of the Holy Spirit, which proclaims *what* He does once we understand the manner in which He works.

GALATIANISM

Galatians is the great epistle that explains to us the doctrine of Galatianism. This is according to the following:

- The Galatians were brought to Christ under Paul's ministry, or at least, one of his associates. This means they were brought in right and given a firm foundation, which was the foundation of the Cross. However, after Paul left and went on to other endeavors and left others in charge, who, incidentally, had very little experience, false teachers came in from Judea, who were attempting to propagate the law. In other words, they believed in Christ, but they gave little significance, if any, to the Cross. In effect, they were telling the believers that to be the type of Christian they ought to be, they had to add the law to their acceptance of Christ. In other words, all the men had to be circumcised, and the little boy babies had to be circumcised at eight days old after they were born.

As well, they had to abide by Sabbath-keeping, etc. That's why Paul bluntly said to them, *"For in Jesus Christ neither circumcision avails anything, nor uncircumcision; but faith which works by love"* (Gal. 5:6).

THE PROBLEM OF THE FLESH

In fact, as the problem of the flesh was the predominant problem with the Galatians, and all others in the early church we might quickly add, it has always been the predominant problem in the church from then and continues to be unto this hour. In fact, I personally believe that it is worse today than ever. So, what did Paul mean by using the term *flesh*?

The word *flesh* in the Greek is *sarx* and can refer to the "meat on the bones of a physical body, or the frailties of human nature," the latter of which is the manner in which Paul used it most. As stated, it is simply the believer attempting to live for God by his own sense, knowledge, personal strength, human ability, etc., which means that this shuts out the Holy Spirit. While the Holy Spirit does not leave the believer in such a situation, still, He can little help us when we're trying to live for God by the means of the flesh.

THE HOLY SPIRIT AND THE FLESH

Now, here is where the great problem ensues: Most Christians don't have the slightest idea how the Holy Spirit works.

Our denominational friends, who do not believe in the baptism with the Holy Spirit with the evidence of speaking with other tongues, just sort of take the Holy Spirit for granted. In fact, they know almost nothing about the Spirit.

Our Pentecostal friends, and I am Pentecostal, are a little more advanced as it regards the Spirit, but not much.

They think that if one is baptized with the Holy Spirit, that is, if they think about it at all, this automatically guarantees the fact that the Holy Spirit will do great and mighty things for them. But yet, we have almost as much moral failure in the ranks of Pentecostals as we do in the other ranks.

So, what is happening here?

It is certainly true that the Holy Spirit comes into the heart and life of the believer at conversion, which is without exception; however, there is a vast difference in being *"born of the Spirit"* and being *"baptized with the Spirit."* If one reads the book of Acts, and the epistles for that matter, it becomes crystal clear that we are expected to go on and be baptized with the Holy Spirit after conversion, which will always be accompanied by speaking with other tongues (Acts 2:4; 10:44-46; 19:1-7).

So, having scripturally settled that, let's go on to the Pentecostals who have been baptized with the Holy Spirit but are still experiencing failure, as are almost all. Why?

KNOWLEDGE

As stated, the Spirit-filled person, not understanding anything about the Cross as it refers to sanctification, which is the manner in which the Holy Spirit works, for the most part, simply takes the Holy Spirit for granted. In fact, there is nothing else he can do, not knowing God's prescribed order of victory.

You should notice that in Romans, Chapters 6, 7, and 8, the words *know, knowing,* or *known,* are used some 11 times. This refers to something that we ought to know, as should be obvious. In these three chapters, it is referring to what the believer ought to know as it regards the Cross of Christ respecting sanctification and how the Holy Spirit works. This is of vital significance, as should be understood.

HOW DOES THE HOLY SPIRIT WORK?

He works strictly from the realm of faith (Gal. 5:6) but with its object ever being the Cross of Christ. In other words, the Cross plays just as much a part in one's sanctification as it does one's salvation, but most Christians don't know that; therefore, they live a defeated life.

Let me say it again: God has only one prescribed order of victory, not 10, not five, not even two — just one. This means that if you do not know that prescribed way, then you are doomed to spiritual failure, no matter how hard you might try otherwise. As stated, due to this gross scriptural ignorance, virtually all of the modern church walks in failure.

As we've already said any number of times in this volume, the Holy Spirit works within our hearts and lives through the legal means of what Jesus did at the Cross, and that demands our faith in the finished work of Christ. That's what the phrase, *"in Christ,"* means, which Paul used some 170 times in his 14 epistles. It means we are in Christ by virtue of what Christ did at the Cross and our faith in that finished work.

THE FINISHED WORK

We simply believe in what Jesus did there, and we speak of the Cross, and in the mind of God, we are literally placed into Christ. That's why Jesus said: *"At that day* (after the Cross and the advent of the Holy Spirit) *you shall know* (there's the word 'know' again) *that I am in My Father, and you in Me, and I in you"* (Jn. 14:20). But we are in Christ only by virtue of the Cross and our faith in that finished work.

Of course, the Holy Spirit is the One who places us in Christ and keeps us in Christ, where we shall ever remain in Christ. However, He does so by virtue of our faith, and more particularly, our faith in the Lord's finished work (Rom. 6:3-14; 8:1-12, 11; Eph. 2:13-18; Gal. 6:14; Col. 2:14-15).

THE RENEWED MIND

Paul said: *"And be not conformed to this world: but be you transformed by the renewing of your mind, that you may prove what is that good, and acceptable, and perfect, will of God"* (Rom. 12:2).

Being conformed to this world refers to the Christian trying to live for God by the same means that the world lives, and we're speaking of one's own personal efforts and strength.

When the mind is transformed, which it must be by being *renewed*, the believer no longer leans on his own strength and ability, but leans totally upon Christ and what Christ has done at the Cross. This enables the Holy Spirit to work mightily within our lives (Rom. 8:13).

Now, most Christians, especially Pentecostals, think they are living by the power of the Holy Spirit simply because they are doing spiritual things. In other words, they heap Scriptures on the flesh, which, incidentally, are wrongly applied, and they think that is *walking after the Spirit*. In reality, they are walking after the flesh (Rom. 8:1).

A PERSONAL EXPERIENCE

The year was 1989, if I remember correctly. I had been invited to preach in a particular church in the state of Florida. Donnie, Frances, and I, along with one of my associates, arrived a day early in order to be at the service that particular night. I was to minister the next night.

The preacher that night preached on *spiritual warfare*.

Incidentally, we've had much preaching on that subject in the last two or three decades, but regrettably, most of the preachers did not have the slightest idea what spiritual warfare was all about.

At any rate, that was his subject that night. His theme was, *"Being militant in Christ."* After he preached his message, he then demonstrated what being militant actually meant.

At that particular time, while I had knowledge as it regarded the Cross for salvation, I really did not understand the Cross at all as it regarded sanctification. However, I did know that what most of the church was doing wasn't right, and I speak of victory over the flesh, etc.

MILITANCY

That preacher's idea of militancy was according to the following: He asked how many people in the building needed help for problems of some particular type. A goodly number of people stepped forward and came to the altar. He, along with other chosen saints, gathered around these people and began to vigorously stomp their feet, make faces, and scream at the Devil as loud as they could. This was supposed to scare the Devil, I suppose, with him then leaving.

I looked at this debacle, and in no way do I intend to demean the motives of the preacher, but I knew this was foolishness.

After a period of time, Frances and I left. Donnie and my associate informed me the next morning that they really rolled into high gear after we left. I suppose our presence hindered them in some manner.

First of all, is there anything in the Bible that substantiates such action? Of course, the answer is *no!* So, where does the church come up with all this foolishness, which runs the gamut from the proverbial A to Z?

GOD'S PRESCRIBED ORDER OF VICTORY

It comes up with all these things simply because it doesn't know God's prescribed order of victory. In other words, it doesn't understand the Cross as the Cross refers to our sanctification and our faith in what Christ did there, which gives the Holy Spirit latitude to work. In fact, what our dear brother was doing was totally and completely of the flesh.

Let me say this: Anything that we do that is not faith in Christ and what Christ has done at the Cross is, in fact, *the flesh.*

Actually, the term *"walking after the flesh"* (Rom. 8:1) simply means to trust in one's own strength and ability, versus *"walking after the Spirit,"* which refers to the Holy Spirit and one's faith being placed in Christ and the Cross. This, of course, refers to His finished work. It's never in things that *we do*, but rather trust and faith in that which *He has already done.*

How many preachers presently know this? There are almost none!

THE GOSPEL

Many preachers preach excellent things *about* the gospel, but they will not be truly preaching the gospel.

Paul said: *"For Christ sent me not to baptize, but to preach the gospel: not with wisdom of words, lest the Cross of Christ should be made of none effect"* (I Cor. 1:17).

This is the reason that I plead with people to get our commentaries and other books and, as well, if possible, to get one or more volumes for preacher friends, or anyone for that matter. In 1997, after some six years of daily seeking His face with tears, the Lord began to open up to me the Message of the Cross. In fact, He began to open it up at that particular time, but with that revelation continuing even unto this hour. I feel that it will ever continue simply because it's impossible to exhaust the finished work of Christ. That's why Paul referred to it as *"the everlasting covenant"* (Heb. 13:20).

What the Lord gave me is not new, not by any means. It is actually what He had already given to Paul, which Paul gave to us. So, what I'm teaching is what Paul taught. However, sadly and regrettably, much of the modern church has no idea what Paul taught; consequently, they are doomed to spiritual failure.

THE REVELATION

I know what it is to try to live for the Lord, and to try with all of my might, but yet, fail simply because I was functioning in the flesh, but did not know that I was functioning in the flesh. That's the tragedy! In looking back, I did not know a single preacher who knew any more then than I did. In other words, they did not understand God's prescribed order of victory. As stated, I understood the Cross as it referred to salvation, but I had no knowledge whatsoever as it referred to sanctification. Consequently, at that time, I tried to live this life as most other Christians do, but it was guaranteed to bring on failure.

We do all types of spiritual things, and we think because these things are spiritual, that's *walking after the Spirit.*

If the believer doesn't understand God's prescribed order, which is the Cross of Christ, such a believer is going to fail. It doesn't matter how hard she or he tries otherwise, the facts are, without the Holy Spirit helping us, within ourselves, we simply are no match for the powers of darkness. The failure may come in many and varied ways, but whatever way it does come, it is always constituted as a *"work of the flesh"* (Gal. 5:19-21).

THE CROSS

It is impossible for the Christian to live above *"works of the flesh,"* if such a Christian doesn't know and understand the Cross as it refers to sanctification.

Paul said, *"But God forbid that I should glory, save in the Cross of our Lord Jesus Christ, by whom the world is crucified unto me, and I unto the world"* (Gal. 6:14).

Paul plainly says here that it is the *Cross* that gives us victory over the world, and remember, he is speaking to believers, not unbelievers.

He also said, *"I am crucified with Christ* (taking us to the Cross)*: nevertheless I live; yet not I, but Christ lives in me: and the life which I now live in the flesh I live by the faith of the Son of God, who loved me, and gave Himself for me"* (Gal. 2:20).

To live a sanctified life, in other words, victory over the world, the flesh, and the Devil, Paul takes us immediately to the Cross by saying, *"I am crucified with Christ."* He is referring to Romans 6:3-5. However, if the believer doesn't understand this, he will try to live this life by his own strength and machinations. As stated, due to the fact that he covers up these machinations with Scriptures, he thinks that he is functioning properly when all the time, he is going in the wrong direction, which will guarantee defeat. He is then left very confused. Let's explain that.

I DO NOT UNDERSTAND

Paul said, *"For that which I do I allow not: for what I would, that do I not; but what I hate, that do I"* (Rom. 7:15).

Romans, Chapter 7, is the story of Paul's experience immediately after he was saved and baptized with the Holy Spirit and, actually, already preaching the gospel. Of course, this was before the Lord gave him understanding as it regarded personal victory.

The apostle tells us that he struggled mightily to live a holy life but found himself failing, despite the fact that he was a new creation in Christ Jesus, despite the fact that he was baptized with the Holy Spirit, and even despite the fact that he was a God-called apostle. So, what was wrong here?

That's what the apostle, in effect, was asking. When he said: *"For that which I do I allow not,"* the word allow should actually have been translated "understand," for that's what it means. He actually said: *"For that which I do I understand not."*

He was trying so hard, and despite his best efforts, he was failing the Lord in some way, which means that at that time, *"lusts of the flesh"* were manifesting themselves in and through him. Sadly, that is the lot presently of almost all Christians.

Please understand, the experiences given in Romans, Chapter 7, are not pertaining to Paul before his conversion, as some think. In fact, a cursory investigation of the language tenses proclaims the fact that Paul was relating his experiences after his conversion.

THE STRUGGLE

Believers struggle, they fight, they labor, they try, and they do so with all their strength, but they find themselves still failing, in fact, with the problem, whatever it might be, getting worse instead of better, despite all their efforts. Paul described it perfectly; they simply don't understand.

I very well know the feeling, for I've been there. Only the Lord knows the number of times that I have shed hot tears, asking the Lord *why*. The answer all the time was in the Word of God, and I refer to Romans, Chapter 6. I thought I understood that chapter, but the truth is, I didn't. Regrettably, there was no one to explain it to me, for the circle in which I traveled did not have understanding either. Since the Lord has given me this revelation, or one might say illumination, regarding the Word of God, looking back, I now know that almost no one in the modern church had proper understanding of this all important subject. Quite possibly, there were some who did, but I was not blessed enough to come across their teaching, whomever they may have been.

Then, when I failed, having the entirety of the church laughing at me, or worse yet, exhibiting pity, it presented itself as about the worst thing that could happen to an individual. Had I not had a firm hold on Christ, I simply could not have survived. Tragically, I had both the news media and the church joining forces, attempting to finish the task of destroying me completely.

I'll never forget the day that I sat with Frances and a group of friends and laid my Bible on the table in front of me and stated, "I don't know the answer, but I know the answer's found in this Book, and by the grace of God, I'm going to find that answer."

And by the grace of God, I did!

THE BELIEVER'S FUNCTION
AND THE BELIEVER'S VICTORY

What I'm about to say, hopefully, will clear up some misunderstanding as it regards the function or calling of a believer and his personal victory. Most Christians don't understand this. They think if God is truly using a person, then this guarantees that such a person has victory in his personal life. It guarantees no such thing!

If God waited until people were perfect before He called them, He simply wouldn't call anyone. In fact, the call of God on a person's life is there from the moment he gives his heart to Christ. It may not materialize for some time, but to be sure, it is there.

All callings are, in effect, *gifts*, which means they are not earned or merited but simply *"gifts from God"* (Eph. 4:11-12). In that gift or function, the Lord will use that individual, and sometimes, use that person mightily.

GOD'S WAY

However, if the individual doesn't go God's way as it regards personal victory, which refers to the Cross, even though the

Lord will have patience for a long while, ultimately and eventually, the function will be hindered by the lack of personal victory. But that in no way means that the good accomplished by this individual, whomever he or she might be, is bogus. In fact, at this very moment, there are tens of thousands of preachers all over the world who are being used of God, with some of them being used mightily, but yet, are failing in some way in their personal lives. Despite their calling, and despite the Holy Spirit helping them greatly to carry out that calling, if they do not know God's prescribed order of victory on a personal basis, they will be living a defeated life. Please understand that they don't have any choice as to how Satan attacks them. Tragically, if the failure is of the type that is scandalous, most of the time, the church will claim that their work is bogus also. Nothing could be further from the truth!

RESTORATION

This is what Paul was talking about when he said: *"Brethren, if a man be overtaken in a fault* (a severe moral fault, for this is what the word means)*, you who are spiritual, restore such an one in the spirit of meekness; considering yourself, lest you also be tempted"* (Gal. 6:1). Regrettably, there aren't many spiritual people around.

The word *spiritual* here simply means that the person is functioning in the realm of the Holy Spirit. What is that realm?

The believer who knows and understands God's prescribed order, which is the Cross of Christ, is to then inform such a believer who has failed as to the reason he failed. What is that reason?

Irrespective as to whom the individual might be, the person has failed simply because he has relied on the *flesh* instead of the *Spirit*. This means that he didn't know God's way and attempted to live this life by his own strength, which, as stated, guarantees failure, despite whatever calling he might have.

The spiritual believer is to lead that person to the Cross, tell him that this is where his faith must be anchored, and where it must remain. This will then give the Holy Spirit latitude to work within his life, which means that he will now be an overcomer instead of one defeated. In other words, he will *be* what he already is in Christ.

REJECTION OF THE CROSS IS NEVER THEOLOGICAL, BUT RATHER MORAL

What if that individual will not accept the Message of the Cross?

Sadly and regrettably, this is the state of many Christians, even preachers.

Sometime back, I had the occasion to invite a particular preacher to be on one of our daily telecasts, *A Study in the Word*. We were teaching exclusively on the Cross. He was present for several programs; however, I could tell that even though he was very readily hearing what was being said, he really was not accepting it. I made mention of this fact to one of my associates after the taping was concluded.

A short time later, my associate was talking with the dear brother, discussing the Cross, when the man said, "This teaching is necessary for some but not for all." In other words, he was saying, "I don't need that particular teaching. I'm doing fine like I am."

The truth is, even though he pastored a good church and, in fact, was doing an excellent work for the Lord, he wasn't doing fine. It came out just a little later that he was struggling with a severe problem within his life, which had been there ever since he was converted. As all such problems, despite his best efforts otherwise, and despite the fact that God was using him, the problem was getting worse and worse. It was finally found out, with his church being destroyed in the process, and as far as I know, he's not even making any attempt now to live for God.

THE MESSAGE OF THE CROSS

Despite all of this, our dear brother is still rejecting, as far as I know, the Message of the Cross. He has chosen to address his problem in another manner, which will do no more good than the young preacher who was stomping his feet and screaming at the Devil, to which we alluded some pages back.

What will happen to this man?

Now that he has been exposed to what Paul taught about the Cross and has rejected it, his situation, despite his best efforts otherwise, will continue to deteriorate unless he repents. If light is rejected, not only do we lose that which we could have had, but we lose what little light we presently have (Mat. 25:28-30).

What do we mean by the statement, "No one rejects the Cross on theological grounds, but rather grounds which are moral"?

To reject something on theological grounds means simply that one doesn't understand the Word, or else, misunderstands the Word. In other words, they think they understand it when, in reality, they don't.

The Message of the Cross is about the simplest message there is. It is so simple that anyone can understand its message. How difficult is the following?

"For God so loved the world, that He gave His only begotten Son, that whosoever believes in Him should not perish, but have everlasting life" (Jn. 3:16). Anyone can understand that!

So, the problem is not theological, but rather moral. What do we mean by *moral*?

We mean that the Cross is rejected because of pride, stubbornness, envy, jealousy, or because of some pet sin we don't want to give up. In other words, there is something morally wrong. The word *moral* refers to anything that is unrighteous.

IGNORANCE OR UNBELIEF

When the Lord first began to give me the revelation of the Cross, my thoughts in those days concerning the majority of the church were that the lack of understanding in this area was the cause of scriptural ignorance. After several years of surveying the situation, I have changed my mind.

While ignorance is certainly true with some, even many, and I speak of scriptural ignorance, in other words, they simply don't know, I have found to my dismay that the major problem, however, is *unbelief*. Perhaps, there is some unbelief even in scriptural ignorance.

Irrespective, the question is put before the church, "Do you believe that what Jesus did at the Cross answers every single problem that humanity might have?"

I was reading a book sometime back that was written by a so-called Christian psychologist. He stated in his book that modern man is facing problems that those in the Bible didn't have to face; consequently, the Bible doesn't hold all the answers for modern man, and he must have the help of humanistic psychology, or words to that effect.

What a travesty! What poppycock! Regrettably, many Christians are following these wolves in sheep's clothing into spiritual oblivion.

GOD HAS GIVEN US ALL THINGS

Concerning the problems that man faces, modern or otherwise, what does the Bible say?

Peter said:

"According as His divine power has given unto us all things that pertain unto life and godliness, through the knowledge of Him who has called us to glory and virtue:

"Whereby are given unto us exceeding great and pre-cious promises: that by these you might be partakers of the divine nature, having escaped the corruption that is in the world through lust" (II Pet. 1:3-4).

Now, either the Lord did give us through Christ and what He did for us at the Cross *all things that pertain unto life and godliness,* or else, the Holy Spirit through Peter didn't tell the truth. I happen to believe that the Holy Spirit through the apostle definitely did tell the truth. You can't have it both ways; He either did or didn't!

PSYCHOLOGY

It is impossible to believe in and promote humanistic psychology while at the same time believing in the Cross of Christ. Either one cancels out the other. Humanistic psy-chology comes purely from the wisdom of man and not at all from God, which means that it is *"earthly, sensual, dev-ilish"* (James 3:15).

But then James said, *"But the wisdom that is from above is first pure* (the Word of God), *then peaceable, gentle, and easy to be entreated, full of mercy and good fruits, without partiality, and without hypocrisy"* (James 3:17).

So, let's say it this way, "Humanistic psychology comes purely from the wisdom of man and not at all from God, as should be obvious." What Jesus did at the Cross alone can address the terrible dilemma in which man now finds himself. That's the reason I grieve when I see the leading Pentecostal denominations, such as the Assemblies of God, the Church of God, and the Foursquare, plus others — at least in the United States and Canada — accepting this nefarious system of the world and actually promoting it as the answer to the ills of man. I think we should look at the Catholic situation.

The Roman Catholic Church is a haven for homosexuals, admitted even by many of its leaders here in the United States and, in fact, the entirety of the world. As such, as we have seen in the news constantly, pedophilia is at pandemic levels.

The Catholics have some of the best psychologists in the world. If this system is plausible, then why hasn't it had more effect in that particular situation? The truth is, it has had no positive effect at all, even as it can have no positive effect at all.

Every soul that's ever been set free, every sin that's ever been washed away, every bondage of darkness that's ever been broken — and it numbers into the hundreds of millions when we look down through the many centuries — all and without exception have been because of Jesus Christ and what He has done for us at the Cross.

So, I have to come to the conclusion, especially as it regards so-called spiritual leaders, that if psychology is promoted, this either shows a gross ignorance of the Word, which should not be the case with so-called leaders, or else, it shows rank unbelief. As I've repeatedly stated, one cannot have it both ways. I have to conclude that the problem is unbelief.

UNBELIEF

What do we mean by the word *unbelief?*

We mean that these religious leaders simply do not believe that what Jesus did at the Cross is the answer to man's dilemma. They rather believe that humanistic psychology is the answer. It's just that simple.

And yet, I thank God that in the recent past, some strong evangelicals, men with a voice, have started speaking out against this nefarious system of humanistic psychology. Regrettably, at least as far as I know, none of these include Pentecostal leaders. So, the adage is true, that which once burned the brightest can dim the lowest, and such are, sadly and regrettably, the Pentecostal denominations.

There would be hope if the leaders of these denominations would admit that what I'm saying is correct. However, sadly, every time in the past when they've read such statements that I've just made or heard me state them publicly, they have only grown more and more incensed, but that is my calling.

In fact, as it regards any true preacher of the gospel, Paul said, *"Preach the Word; be instant in season, out of season; reprove, rebuke* (and this is what I'm trying to do), *exhort with all longsuffering and doctrine.*

"For the time will come when they will not endure sound doctrine; but after their own lusts shall they heap to themselves teachers, having itching ears;

"And they shall turn away their ears from the truth, and shall be turned unto fables" (II Tim. 4:2-4).

Humanistic psychology falls into the category of *fables*.

CONFLICT

"And Moses said unto Joshua, Choose us out men, and go out, fight with Amalek: tomorrow I will stand on the top of the hill with the rod of God in my hand" (Ex. 17:9).

At the new birth, the divine nature is imparted to the believing sinner (II Pet. 1:4). This new nature is created by the Holy Spirit; the *"seed"* (I Jn. 3:9) used is the Word of God.

When the new nature is communicated by God to the one born again, the old sinful nature remains and, in effect, remains unchanged as far as its character is concerned. It will be unchanged accordingly till death or the coming of Christ when it will be destroyed. The Scripture says that at this particular time, *"this corruptible* (the sinful nature) *must put on incorruption* (nothing left but the divine nature)*"* (I Cor. 15:53).

However, the power of the sin nature presently is definitely broken, with the guilt removed (Rom. 6:6-7).

In the Christian, in fact, in every Christian, there are two conflicting natures: One sinful, the other sinless; one born of the flesh, the other born of God. These two natures differ from each other in origin, in character, in disposition, and in the activities they produce. They have nothing in common. In fact, they are bitterly opposed to each other. This is what is in view typically in the second half of Exodus, Chapter 17, the chapter of our study.

However, there is a way provided by the Lord, which we will address momentarily, that will give us continuous victory over the sin nature, with it, in effect, causing us no problem. Actually, even though it still remains in the Christian, it is supposed to be dormant and, in fact, will be dormant if it is addressed after the Spirit (Rom. 6:11, 14).

JACOB

There are many types respecting this in the Old Testament, but one of the most illustrated is Jacob. In effect, he had two names: One which he received from his earthly parents and one which he received from God.

At the great wrestling match with God (Gen. 32:28), the Lord gave him the new name of Israel, which means, "prince of God" or "soldier of God." From that point onward, the history of Jacob presents a series of strange paradoxes. His life exhibited a dual personality, which, in a sense, is characteristic of every believer.

At one moment, we see him trusting God with implicit confidence; at another, we behold him giving way to an evil heart of unbelief — and it is unbelief which seems to characterize the major problems.

If the Bible student will read carefully Chapters 33 through 49 of Genesis, he will notice how that sometimes the

Holy Spirit refers to the patriarch as Jacob and at other times as Israel. When Jacob is referred to, it is the activities of the "old nature" that are in view; when Israel is mentioned, it is the fruits of the "new nature" that are evidenced.

THE NEW NATURE

For example, when Joseph's brethren returned to their father from Egypt and told him that his favorite son was yet alive and was now governor over all the land of Egypt, we are told that *"Jacob's heart fainted, for he believed them not"* (Gen. 45:26). But when *"they told him all the words of Joseph, which he had said unto them: and when he saw the wagons which Joseph had sent to carry him, the spirit of Jacob their father revived: and 'Israel' said, It is enough; Joseph my son is yet alive!"* (Gen. 45:27-28).

It is also very interesting to note the closing words concerning the patriarch. It is as follows:

"When 'Jacob' had made an end of commanding his sons, he gathered up his feet into the bed, and yielded up the ghost (spirit) *... And the physicians embalmed 'Israel!'"* (Gen. 49:33; 50:2).

Jacob died; *Israel* was embalmed. This means that at death, only the "new nature" will be preserved.

However, that which we wish to emphasize is that during the Christian's life on earth, there is a conflict between the two natures.

Paul said, *"The flesh lusts against the Spirit, and the Spirit against the flesh: and these are contrary the one to the other: so that you cannot do the things that you would"* (Gal. 5:17).

HOW CAN THE OLD NATURE BE TOTALLY SUBDUED?

What we are addressing here, we have already answered in detail, even several times. However, due to the fact that it seems to be so difficult for many believers to understand — and I continue to speak of the dual between the two natures and how victory is obtained — it is incumbent upon me to state the same truth over and over if I have to in order that all may understand. As we shall see, this is the area that Satan fights the Christian the hardest, and regrettably, it is the area that most Christians understand the least. That is tragic because it leads to tragic consequences.

Considering that this is the single most important thing for the believer to learn, and considering that so few modern believers have any understanding at all of this of which we speak, we then learn the reason for defeated lives. It doesn't matter who the person is, as we've already said any number of times in this volume. If the believer doesn't know and understand God's prescribed order of victory, and we speak of victory over the sin nature, then such a person is doomed to spiritual failure, and the spiritual failure will continue to get worse and worse.

JESUS CHRIST IS THE SOURCE

The following is God's way and, in fact, His only way: That it may be more understandable, we might say that Jesus Christ is the source of all things that we receive from God (Jn. 1:1-3, 29; 14:6, 20).

Jesus Christ is the One who has paid the price at Calvary's Cross. In fact, He is the only leader of a religion, so to speak, who claimed to be God and, in fact, was and is God.

Actually, Christianity is not a religion, but rather a relationship with a person, the Lord Jesus Christ.

Before the foundation of the world, through foreknowledge, God knew that He would create this planet and the universe, as well as create man, and that man would fall. At that time in eternity past, it was determined by the Godhead that man would be redeemed by God becoming man for the express purpose of going to the Cross, where the holiness of God could forever be satisfied, which He did. Jesus Christ is the Saviour, the baptizer with the Holy Spirit, the healer, and He is all in all.

To be frank, Jesus Christ is the key to the throne of God. As someone has well said, if someone or even an entire religious denomination gets everything right except *who Jesus is* and *what Jesus did*, then nothing they do can actually be right. Jesus Christ is all in all.

THE CROSS OF CHRIST IS THE MEANS

With Jesus as our source, we must understand that the means by which all these wonderful things are given to us is the Cross of Christ. In other words, it is the Cross and what Jesus there did that makes everything possible (Rom. 6:1-14; I Cor. 1:17-18, 23; 2:2; Col. 2:10-15).

Of course, when we speak of the Cross, we aren't speaking of the wooden beam on which Jesus died, but rather what He there accomplished. To understand all of this, we must understand who Jesus is, God manifest in the flesh, and what He did, which was the giving of Himself as a sacrifice on the Cross. It is who He is and what He did! This means that every single thing we receive from the Lord, the Cross of Christ has made it all possible. That's the reason it's so wrong for the believer to try to gain victory outside of the Cross. In fact, such cannot be done. It all can be summed up in the one phrase, *"Jesus Christ and Him crucified."*

THE CROSS MUST BE THE OBJECT OF OUR FAITH

In other words, we must understand that the Cross of Christ is the means by which we are given everything, which makes it the object of our faith. Once again, we aren't speaking of the wooden beam on which Jesus died, but rather what He there did. The Cross of Christ has made everything possible, and as such, this is where our faith must be anchored. When one has one's faith exclusively in Christ and the Cross, this means that we have it in the Word of God. In fact, the story of the Bible from Genesis 1:1 through Revelation 22:21 is the story of *Jesus Christ and Him crucified.*

THE HOLY SPIRIT

With Christ as our source, the Cross as our means, and the Cross as the object of our faith, which is so very, very important, then the Holy Spirit — who works exclusively within the parameters, so to speak, of the finished work of Christ — will gloriously and grandly help us (Rom. 8:1-11; Eph. 2:13-18; Acts 1:9).

What we have given you is God's way not only of redemption but, as well, of sanctification, in other words, how we live for God, how we order our behavior, and how we have victory over the world, the flesh, and the Devil. We are no match within ourselves against the powers of darkness. It is the Holy Spirit alone who can do what needs to be done. The Holy Spirit is God, and of course, that means that He is omnipotent, omniscient, and omnipresent.

What I have given you above is God's way of life, living, and victory in every capacity. As we have previously stated, the Lord doesn't have five ways, not even two ways, but only one, and that is *Jesus Christ and Him crucified.*

If the believer thinks he can do this thing another way, he has just thrown in his lot with Cain, who determined to do things his way instead of God's way. Let the reader understand, God's way is the Cross of Christ. If that sacrifice is rejected, which is the Cross of Christ, then the one offering another sacrifice is rejected as well. If the sacrifice, and we speak of Christ crucified, is accepted, and it always will be, then the one offering the sacrifice is accepted. God doesn't so much look at the one submitting the sacrifice as He does the sacrifice being submitted.

Everything is in the sacrifice.

THE POWER OF GOD

Paul said, *"For the preaching of the Cross is to them who perish foolishness; but unto us who are saved it is the power of God"* (I Cor. 1:18).

The power of God is not in the Cross itself, and we speak of the wooden beam, and it's certainly not in the death that Jesus died, but in reality, it's in what that death provided.

The death of Christ was a sacrifice, which means that He freely offered up His own life, was accepted by God as payment for all sin, past, present, and future, at least for all who will believe. With the terrible sin debt being lifted— and done so by the *"last Adam"* (I Cor. 15:45-50)—the way was then cleared for the Holy Spirit, who is God, to take up abode in the heart and life of all believers, and to do so on a permanent basis (Jn. 14:16-17; I Cor. 3:16). The power is in the Holy Spirit, as should be obvious (Acts 1:8), and this is the key to everything. However, He works exclusively, as stated, within the boundaries of the finished work of Christ. In other words, the sacrifice of Christ made possible all that the Holy Spirit does. In fact, there is every scriptural evidence that the Holy Spirit actually superintended the death of Christ.

The Scripture says: *"How much more shall the blood of Christ, who through the eternal Spirit offered Himself without spot to God, purge your conscience from dead works to serve the living God?"* (Heb. 9:14).

DEAD WORKS

In this one verse of Scripture just quoted, we are told how the flesh may be subdued.

As the Spirit of God superintended the death of Christ, He did so that every single thing may be done perfectly, which it was. Through that sacrifice, and that sacrifice alone, can we purge our conscience from dead works in order to serve the living God.

As well, the phrase, *"Who through the eternal Spirit offered Himself without spot to God,"* completely refutes the Jesus died spiritually doctrine.

How could Christ die spiritually, which means to be bereft of God and means that He died as a sinner, and at the same time, *"offer Himself without spot to God"*?

Then Paul said, *"And for this cause He* (Christ) *is the mediator of the New Testament* (new covenant), *that by means of death (the death of the Cross), for the redemption of the transgressions that were under the first Testament* (old covenant), *they which are called might receive the promise of eternal inheritance"* (Heb. 9:15).

This passage tells us that the death of Christ not only addressed itself to all who lived then and forward but, as well, to all of the Old Testament saints. That's why Jesus could liberate all of these saints from Paradise, where they had been held captive by Satan, and then take them with Him to Glory, where they are presently (Eph. 4:8-10).

Now, when believers die, they instantly go to be with Christ (Phil. 1:23). This time frame spans everything from the Cross unto the present and will definitely continue.

THE AMALEKITES

Considering how precious water was and is, as it regards the desert, and considering that a veritable river was gushing out of the rock, the Amalekites attacked Israel, thinking to take possession of this tremendous river.

The Scripture says, *"Then came Amalek and fought with Israel."* The Holy Spirit has called our attention to the time when this occurred. It was when Moses smote the rock, and the waters gushed out.

Then, for the first time, Israel was called upon to do some fighting. They had done no fighting in the house of bondage, nor had the Lord called upon them to fight the Egyptians at the Red Sea. But now that this which typified the Holy Spirit had been given, their warfare commenced. It was that which typified the Holy Spirit that caused the Amalekites to attack Israel! Wonderfully accurate is the type.

All of this corresponds with the believer's struggle, and how it is to be carried out, even as we shall see in the following verses.

The reception of the Holy Spirit immediately causes war. Up to this point, God had fought for them, but the command now was that they go out and fight.

As we've already stated, there is an immense difference between justification and sanctification. The one is Christ fighting *for* us; the other, the Holy Spirit fighting *in* us. The entrance of the new nature is the beginning of warfare with the old.

JUSTIFICATION BY FAITH

Paul plainly said, *"Therefore being justified by faith, we have peace with God through our Lord Jesus Christ"* (Rom. 5:1).

Justification in the Greek, as a noun, is *dikaiosis* or *dikaioma*. As a verb it is *dikaioo*.

Basically, all three words denote the act of one being pronounced righteous because of acquittal from all guilt. All that was necessary on God's part for our justification has been effected in the death of Christ. On this account, as well, He was raised from the dead. That God justifies the believing sinner on the ground of Christ's death and that sinner's faith in Christ involves His free gift of life.

To make it simple to understand, righteousness is *what God has declared to be right.*

The manner in which one is declared righteous by God is by and through faith evidenced on the part of the believing sinner toward Christ and what Christ has done for us at the Cross. There is nothing that the believing sinner can do to justify himself. There is no price that he can pay and no merit that he can come by, with it all being strictly by faith.

This is exactly what the Lord was speaking of when He said, *"For God so loved the world, that He gave His only begotten Son, that whosoever believes in Him should not perish, but have everlasting life"* (Jn. 3:16).

HOW DOES GOD JUSTIFY A BELIEVING SINNER?

He does so on the basis of the sacrificial, atoning death of Christ and the believing sinner's faith in Christ.

The question might be asked as to how a perfectly righteous God can declare an obviously guilty sinner to be righteous and justify his actions.

It is all done in Christ. Jesus paid the price for man's redemption by going to the Cross and offering up Himself as a sacrifice, which He did. Whenever the believing sinner evidences faith in Christ and asks for pardon on the basis of the death of Christ on the Cross, God will instantly pardon such a sinner and will cleanse him or her from all sin and, thereby, declare such a person to be perfectly righteous. As stated, it is all done in Christ and one's simple faith in Christ and what He did for us at the Cross.

No fault is found with such a person, irrespective of what his past life has been, simply because his righteousness is based solely on Christ and what Christ has done at the Cross. When the Lord justifies one, as He does every single person who comes to Him, He justifies totally and completely. There is no such thing as a partial justification. One is either completely justified or not justified at all!

To be brief, anyone can come to the Lord if he so desires, and all who come will be washed and cleansed and declared perfectly righteous. The Scripture plainly says, *"For whosoever shall call upon the name of the Lord shall be saved (i.e., 'shall be justified')"* (Rom. 10:13).

SANCTIFICATION BY FAITH

Justification is one's standing, and sanctification is one's *state.*

In essence, one is perfectly sanctified the moment one comes to Christ. Paul said, *"And such were some of you: but you are washed, but you are sanctified, but you are justified in the name of the Lord Jesus, and by the Spirit of our God"* (I Cor. 6:11).

In fact, one must be washed clean, which means to *"be made righteous,"* before one can be justified, which means *"to be declared righteous."*

However, the sanctification to which we have addressed ourselves here, which means to be set apart solely for Christ, has to do with the justification process and, as well, falls into the category of our *standing.* In other words, God can accept nothing except perfection. This means that we are sanctified and justified on the premise of the perfection of Christ, which refers to what He did for us at the Cross as a perfect sacrifice. However, there is a part to our sanctification that refers to our state. *Our standing* never wavers, while our *state* is somewhat up and down.

Paul addressed this particular act of sanctification in this manner. He said, *"And the very God of peace sanctify you wholly; and I pray God your whole spirit and soul and body be preserved blameless unto the coming of our Lord Jesus Christ"* (I Thess. 5:23).

OUR STATE AND OUR STANDING

In essence, Paul is saying that the Holy Spirit wants to bring our *state* up to our *standing*. In other words, He wants us to *be* what we actually *are*.

This is where the struggle comes in. This is what the Holy Spirit is proclaiming to us in this latter portion of Chapter 17, using Amalek as an example. This is where the Christian has his greatest problem. This is what I'm talking about when I say that the modern church understands the Cross somewhat as it refers to salvation, but almost none at all as it refers to sanctification. As we've already explained, the believer must understand that his faith had to *be placed* in the Cross in order to be saved, and that it must *remain* in the Cross, that is, if we are to live a sanctified life.

As it regards justification, sanctification is a once-for-all work as it regards our everyday living. It is, however, also a progressive work. As stated, the Holy Spirit, who is the sanctifying agent, is constantly attempting to bring our *state* up to our *standing*. This is where Satan fights us the hardest, and this is where the Holy Spirit fights for us the hardest. However, He can fight for us only on the grounds of our faith being properly placed, which always refers to the Cross of Christ.

If the believer will place his or her faith exclusively in Christ and what Christ has done for us at the Cross, and maintain it exclusively in Christ and the Cross, the Holy Spirit — who is God, who can do anything, and who works exclusively within the parameters, so to speak, of the finished work of Christ — will then work mightily on our behalf.

That's what Jesus was talking about when He said, *"If any man will come after Me* (the criteria for discipleship)*, let him deny himself* (not asceticism as many think, but rather that one denies one's own willpower, self-will, personal strength, and ability, depending totally on Christ)*, and take up his cross* (the benefits of the Cross, looking exclusively to what Jesus did there to meet our every need) *daily* (this is so important, our looking to the Cross; that we must renew our faith in what Christ has done for us, even on a daily basis, for Satan will ever try to move us away from the Cross as the object of our faith, which always spells disaster)*, and follow Me* (Christ can be followed only by the believer looking to the Cross, understanding what it accomplished, and by that means alone [Rom. 6:1-14; 8:1-11; I Cor. 1:17-18, 21, 23; 2:2; Gal. 6:14; Col. 2:10-15]).

"For whosoever will save his life shall lose it (try to live one's life outside of Christ and the Cross)*: but whosoever will lose his life for My sake, the same shall save it* (when we place our faith entirely in Christ and the Cross, looking exclusively to Him, we have just found 'more abundant life' [Jn. 10:10])*"* (Lk. 9:23-24).

SELF SANCTIFICATION

Not understanding the Cross of Christ as it refers to sanctification, most believers attempt to sanctify themselves. They try to do so by various means. Some think they can fast their way to sanctification, while others use other methods. None works because none are scriptural, at least in that capacity. Of course, fasting is scriptural, etc., but to sanctify oneself is not!

All one has to do is place one's faith exclusively in Christ and the Cross, and maintain it exclusively in Christ and the Cross, even as Jesus said, on a daily basis. That being done, as we've already stated, the Holy Spirit will grandly help such a believer and will help him to live the sanctified life, which is *more abundant life.*

Christianity is the greatest experience in the world, but only if we do it God's way. When we try to sanctify ourselves by our own machinations, failure is guaranteed, which brings condemnation and misery. Unfortunately, virtually the entirety of the body of Christ presently is living in a state of spiritual failure because of not understanding what we are here teaching. In other words, it is impossible for a believer to sanctify himself, irrespective as to what he does. By doing it God's way, which is the way of the Cross and only requires faith, then we will find a victory that is beyond our greatest comprehension.

JOSHUA

"So Joshua did as Moses had said to him, and fought with Amalek: and Moses, Aaron, and Hur went up to the top of the hill" (Ex. 17:10).

The person who isn't born again knows absolutely nothing of the conflict between the two natures of the individual or of the abiding sense of inward corruption that this experience conveys. The unregenerate man is entirely under the dominion of the flesh; he serves its lusts, and he does its will. In fact, the flesh doesn't fight its subjects; it rules over them. However, as soon as we receive the new nature, the conflict begins.

It should be understood that Israel did not attack Amalek, but rather Amalek attacked Israel. To correspond with this, note how that in Galatians 5:17, it is first said that *"the flesh lusts against the spirit"* and not vice versa.

Some pages back, we explained to you what the *flesh* actually is and what it means to be *in the flesh*. So now, let us note carefully how Israel actually engaged Amalek as it regarded this conflict.

A MAN OF GREAT FAITH

As the water out of the rock was a great type, likewise, Amalek and how he was opposed presents another great type. In fact, Chapter 17 of Exodus portrays the entirety of the plan of God.

Israel was without water, signifying the lost condition of mankind and the inability of this world to change that condition.

The smitten rock portrays Calvary, which is God's solution for sin and sinners. Now we have His prescription for victory.

Joshua now made his entrance. He would prove to be one of the greatest men of God who ever lived. In the correct pronunciation, he is *Joshua ben Nun*, which means "Joshua son of Nun." His name means "salvation" and, in fact, he is a type of Christ. As well, the name *Jesus*, as it refers to our Saviour, which is the Greek derivative, is actually *Joshua* in Hebrew. So, Jesus was known by the name of *Joshua*.

Moses chose him as a personal assistant and gave him command of a detachment from the as yet unorganized tribes to repel the raiding Amalekites.

We will find that Joshua was a man of great faith. As the Ephraimite representative on the reconnaissance from Kadesh (Num., Chpts. 13-14), he backed Caleb's recommendation to go ahead with the invasion. As a result, he and Caleb escaped the curse leveled by God on the unbelieving people, who refused to go in at that time.

In the plains by the Jordan, he was formally consecrated as Moses' successor as it regarded the leadership of the children of Israel.

JOSHUA AS A TYPE OF CHRIST

Joshua was a conqueror. He was selected here by Moses to fight the Amalekites just as he would fight Israel's enemies in the Promised Land some 40 years later. As he conquered Israel's foes, Christ has conquered our foes. As should be obvious, Joshua, in this capacity as a *type*, is very, very important. In fact, this is where the believer has his greatest problem. If he doesn't understand Christ and what Christ has done for us, then he will try all over again to do the work that Christ has already done and, in fact, that which he cannot do any way.

In other words, such a direction is guaranteed of defeat, but regrettably, that's where most Christians presently are.

To address an extremely complicated subject, and do so briefly, is not a simple task; however, that's what we will attempt to do here.

VICTORY IS ONLY IN CHRIST

Let's say it another way because the following must be understood: God does not give victory to fallen man; He gives victory alone to His Son and our Saviour, the Lord Jesus Christ. To obtain the victory, we must enter into Christ, which is done by faith (Rom. 6:3-5, 11, 14), but this is Christian man's greatest problem.

Man attempts to gain the victory in all types of ways other than the Cross, all without success.

WHAT DO WE MEAN BY VICTORY?

Pure and simple, we are referring to victory over sin. Satan tries to pull the believer into sin in some fashion. It may be sins of the spirit or sins of the flesh; nevertheless, it is sin, and all sin is terribly destructive and that which God cannot abide.

The church faces this problem in all types of ways. Our Word of Faith friends claim that sin is no longer a problem for the believer simply because he is a new creation in Christ, in effect, the righteousness of God; therefore, sin is no longer a problem. He is instructed to never mention sin, for in so doing, they claim, such will develop a sin consciousness, which is detrimental to the new creation man.

Of course, there is some truth in what they say, even as most lies contain some truth. We are a new creation and, therefore, the righteousness of God (II Cor. 5:17, 21). However, if sin is no longer a problem, then the Holy Spirit wasted an awful lot of space instructing believers through the Apostle Paul on how to have victory over sin.

No! Sin is definitely the problem, in fact, the main problem by far. Ignoring sin or claiming it doesn't exist does not change its status or effect.

It is certainly true that the believer should dwell on Christ and certainly not on sin; however, Paul also said, *"Lest Satan should get an advantage of us: for we are not ignorant of his devices"* (II Cor. 2:11). Regrettably, because of false teaching, many, if not most, Christians are ignorant of Satan's devices.

So, when we speak of *victory*, we're speaking of victory over the world, the flesh, and the Devil. John the Beloved said: *"This is the victory that overcomes the world, even our faith"* (I Jn. 5:4).

SHOULD WE CONFESS OUR SINS TO THE LORD?

Unfortunately, there is a teaching making headway in the body of Christ presently, which states that due to the fact that Jesus atoned for all sin, past, present, and future, this means the believer is to never mention sin. If he sins, he doesn't have to confess it to Christ, they say, but just ignore it.

While it is certainly true that our Lord has most definitely atoned for all sin, past, present, and future, at least for all who will believe, in no way does that mean that we are not to confess our sins to the Lord.

John the Beloved wrote, *"If we say that we have no sin* (refers to 'the sin nature'), *we deceive ourselves* (refers to self-deception), *and the truth is not in us.* (This does not refer to all truth as it regards believers, but rather that the truth of the indwelling sinful nature is not in us.)

"If we confess our sins (pertains to acts of sin, whatever they might be; the sinner is to believe [Jn. 3:16]; the saint is to confess), *He* (the Lord) *is faithful and just to forgive us our sins* (God will always be true to His own nature and promises, keeping faith with Himself and with man), *and to cleanse us from all unrighteousness.* ('All,' not some. All sin was remitted, paid for, and put away on the basis of the satisfaction offered for the demands of God's holy law, which sinners broke when the Lord Jesus died on the Cross)" (I Jn. 1:8-9).

John then wrote: *"My little children, these things write I unto you, that you sin not.* (This presents the fact that the Lord saves us from sin, not in sin. This passage tells us that as believers, we don't have to sin. Victory over sin is found exclusively in the Cross.) *And if any man sin, we have an advocate with the Father, Jesus Christ the righteous* (Jesus is now seated at the right hand of the Father, signifying that His mission is complete, and His very presence guarantees intercession [Heb. 7:25-26; 9:24; 10:12]):

"*And He is the propitiation* (satisfaction) *for our sins: and not for ours only, but also for the sins of the whole world.* (This pertains to the fact that the satisfaction is as wide as the sin. If men do not experience its benefit, the fault is not in its efficacy, but in man himself)" (I Jn. 2:1-2).

The advocates of the *no confession* claim state that Chapter 1 of I John was written to unbelievers and not to believers, hence, confession of sin demanded, etc.

Even a cursory investigation of Chapter 1 of Saint John disproves such thinking.

In the first place, there is nowhere in the Bible that it tells the unredeemed to confess their sins. How could they do such when we're speaking of thousands upon thousands of sins. No, the Holy Spirit through John is here speaking to believers, as is overly obvious.

THE SEVEN CHURCHES OF ASIA

In the addressing of the seven churches of Asia, our Lord intended for these messages to be for the entirety of the church and for all time. I think anyone would have to admit that these seven messages to these seven churches are to believers. To five of these churches, He demanded repentance, which is a confession of sin (Rev. 2:5, 16, 21; 3:3, 19).

I hardly think that our Lord would have demanded repentance of five of the churches if it was wrong for a believer to confess his sins to the Lord.

THE GREATEST PRAYER OF REPENTANCE

Psalm 51 is the greatest prayer of repentance that has ever been offered. It typifies the following:

- It is a prayer of David confessing his sin before the Lord and asking for mercy and grace because of his sin of adultery with Bath-sheba and the murder of her husband Uriah.
- This prayer typifies the prayer that Israel will pray at the close of the great tribulation during the battle of Armageddon, when it looks like she will surely be totally destroyed by the Antichrist. Then she will cry to God, who will most definitely hear her, which will instigate the second coming.
- Above all, this is the intercessory prayer of Christ on behalf of all who cry to Him for mercy and grace. When a believer sins and confesses that sin before the Lord, our Lord doesn't really have to do anything, with it already having been done at the Cross. His very presence at the throne of God tells us that God has accepted His sacrifice of Himself and, therefore, His

very presence guarantees forgiveness of all sins that are confessed by believers.

The following is what David said: *"Have mercy upon me, O God, according to Your lovingkindness: according unto the multitude of Your tender mercies blot out my transgressions"* (Ps. 51:1).

He then said, *"Wash me throughly from mine iniquity, and cleanse me from my sin"* (Ps. 51:2).

And then, *"For I acknowledge my transgressions: and my sin is ever before me"* (Ps. 51:3).

"Hide Your face from my sins, and blot out all my iniquities" (Ps. 51:9).

In fact, as we have previously stated, the entirety of Psalm 51 is the greatest prayer of repentance known to man. To be sure, David confessed his sin before the Lord just as we have to confess our sins before the Lord.

WHAT GOOD DOES IT DO US TO CONFESS OUR SINS?

First of all, let's state that for the believer to confess his sins before the Lord, he doesn't have to go into a ritual or a ceremony, or call a preacher, etc. In fact, all he has to do is confess these sins in his heart to the Lord, wherever he might be, and to be sure, forgiveness will be instant.

- Confessing our sins before the Lord states that we have sinned.

- It lets us know how bad that sin really is, at least as much as a poor human being can understand such.

- Confessing our sin before the Lord, whatever it might be — that is, if we have sinned — admits our failure and the fact that we are responsible.

- While the Lord is merciful and gracious and does not leave immediately, if confession of sin is ignored, to be sure, such a person will grow weaker as time goes by. This is because what is being done — refusal to confess our sins to the Lord — is within itself a sin. It is a disobedience of the Word of God. A lack of confession will open the door for the sin to be continued, even on an increasing basis, which is the sure road to disaster. No believer wants to sin, and when sin is committed, the heavy weight of that transgression is upon us until we confess it before the Lord, where forgiveness and fellowship are restored.

IS SIN UNFORGIVEN THAT IS UNCONFESSED?

Yes, it is! Sin cannot be forgiven until the believer admits that he has sinned, confesses his sin before the Lord, and asks for mercy and grace. Let's go once again to the great 51st Psalm.

David said, *"Make me to hear joy and gladness; that the bones which You have broken may rejoice"* (Ps. 51:8). The notes from The Expositor's Study Bible regarding this Scripture say:

"Forgiveness for the past never exhausts the fullness of pardon. There is provision for the future. The expression, 'bones which You have broken,' presents a figure of speech meaning that one cannot proceed until things have been made right with God. It is as though a man's leg is broken, and he cannot walk. Unforgiven sin immobilizes the soul the same as a broken bone immobilizes the body."

No, this strange doctrine that says that believers never have to confess their sins to the Lord, and, in fact, shouldn't, is not biblical, and if continued, will lead to hurt and possibly even wreckage and ruin. The Lord does not leave us immediately when we do wrong, even when we refuse to confess our wrongdoing. Still, wrongdoing has to be corrected in some way, and if it is not, there will be a spiritual deterioration.

IN CHRIST

There was no way that man could extricate himself from his terrible dilemma that was brought upon him by the fall in the garden of Eden. Cut off from God, man was spiritually dead, and dead means dead. This means that he had no concept of God, didn't understand God, and in no way could have had any feelings toward God, at least while in this terrible state.

So, if man was to be delivered from this dilemma, God would have to take the initiative, which He did, and at a fearsome price. God would become man, which is referred to as the *"incarnation."* However, just to become man was not enough; He had to be a perfect man. Consequently, He would have to be born of a virgin, for to be born otherwise would place Him in the position of all other men, for in Adam, all died (I Cor. 15:22).

So, Christ was born of the Virgin Mary, which means He was born without the taint of original sin. This means that He didn't have a sin nature.

In His earthly life, Jesus' walk was perfect in every capacity, with Him not sinning in word, thought, or deed. He had to do this in order to be our substitute man. That's why Paul referred to Him as the *"second man"* (I Cor. 15:47). The first man, Adam, failed; the second man, Christ, succeeded on every count.

UNDER THE LAW

Jesus was born under the law (Gal. 4:4), for the law, and we speak of the law of Moses, was the righteousness demanded by God of man. Man could not attain to this righteousness simply because of his fallen state, but Jesus would attain to this righteousness by keeping the law perfectly in every respect. He would do so as our representative man, and it would all be done on our behalf. In other words, every single thing He did, and I mean in every capacity, was done exclusively for us and not at all for Himself.

Even though He kept the law perfectly, there still remained the most critical aspect, which was the law that had been broken by all of humanity. This had to be addressed and, in fact, was the very purpose and reason for which Christ came. While everything that Christ did was of utmost significance, the main purpose of His coming was to serve as a sacrifice (I Pet. 1:18-20).

So, Christ has already done every single thing for us that we couldn't do for ourselves, and we obtained His victory — which He desired to give us, and for which He died — by evidencing faith in Him and what He did for us at the Cross. We are not to try to fight these battles all over again, but rather to trust in the victory that He has already won, and did so in totality.

OBEYING THE WORD

Every Christian is to obey the Word of God. In effect, that's not a question but, in fact, that which is obvious. However, it's the manner in which we go about obeying the Word that is brought into view.

So, how does one obey the Word?

Most Christians would retort by simply saying, "Just simply do what it says to do!"

That is correct, but it leaves much to be desired. We come back to our original question, "How do we do what we're supposed to do as it regards the Word of God?"

If the Christian sets out by his own efforts, intuition, ability, strength, and machinations to obey the Word, no matter how sincere he might be, no matter how studious he might be, and no matter how zealous he might be, the end result will never be victory but always failure. In other words, he will do the very thing that he's trying not to do, which is to disobey the Word.

Paul brought this out very succinctly in Romans, Chapter 7. He said, *"For that which I do I allow* (understand) *not: for what I would* (desire to do), *that do I not; but what I hate* (fail the Lord), *that do I"* (Rom. 7:15).

FAITH IN CHRIST AND THE CROSS

So, we learn from Romans, Chapter 7, that one cannot obey the Word by simply desiring to do so. In fact, it is impossible to obey in that manner.

We obey the Word by doing the very same thing that I've been telling you to do throughout the entirety of this volume. We are to understand that Christ has already done all of this for us. He alone has perfectly obeyed the Word.

It is said of Christ: *"I have not departed from Your judgments: for You have taught me"* (Ps. 119:102).

When we evidence simple faith in Him, which refers to what He did for us at the Cross, the Holy Spirit then works strongly and mightily through us. He always works within the parameters of the finished work of Christ, and then we become *"doers of the Word,"* and not merely *"hearers of the Word"* (James 1:22).

So, our heavenly Joshua has already fought and won all the battles, and we enter into His victory by simply having faith in Him and what He did, which refers to the Cross (Rom. 6:1-14; 8:1-11; I Cor. 1:17-18, 21, 23; 2:2, 5; Gal. 6:14; Eph. 2:13-18; Col. 2:10-15; I Pet. 1:18-20).

We are never told in the Bible to fight the Devil, at least not in the sense of which most people think. We are told rather to *"fight the good fight of faith"* (I Tim. 6:12).

While we do wrestle with the cohorts of Satan, and we, of course, speak of spiritual conflict, it is the manner that we address this which decides the difference (Eph. 3:10-18). We do it by simple faith in Christ and the finished work of the Cross.

MOSES

In this scenario, Moses is a type of the body of Christ. The *"rod of God"* that he held in his hand was a type of victory over the serpent. Remember the rod turning into a serpent (Ex. 4:2-4)? This is the believer's problem, not a lack of education, finances, or social graces, but rather sin and its destructive power caused by Satan and that world of spiritual darkness. Aaron was the head of Israel's priesthood, and so speaks plainly of our Great High Priest, the Lord Jesus Christ.

Hur (Vs. 10) means "light" — the emblem of divine holiness — and so points to the Holy Spirit of God. Thus, God in His grace has fully provided for us.

"Likewise the Spirit also helps our infirmities: for we know not what we should pray for as we ought: but the Spirit itself (Himself) *makes intercession for us with groan-*

ings which cannot be uttered" (Rom. 8:26). This is the earthly side represented by Hur.

The heavenly side, represented by Aaron, speaks of Christ as the messenger of the covenant coming and standing at the altar, having a golden censor, *"and there was given unto him much incense, that he should offer it with the prayers of all saints upon the golden altar which was before the throne"* (Rev. 8:3). The *"hill"* represented Calvary, where all of this was accomplished.

So, Joshua, who represented Christ, was fighting the Amalekites, who represented the world, the flesh, and the Devil. Moses represented all believers, and Aaron represented Christ and His position as Great High Priest. Hur represented the Holy Spirit, and, as stated, the *"hill"* represented the Cross.

PREVAILED

"And it came to pass, when Moses held up his hand, that Israel prevailed: and when he let down his hand, Amalek prevailed" (Ex. 17:11).

Moses holding up his hands toward Heaven, with probably the rod of God in one of them, or maybe in both of them, signified that all help comes from above. We need to take very seriously this *"type"* set before us because it is a perfect example of our means of victory even now.

If it is to be noticed, when he let down his hands, *"Amalek prevailed."* Hands upraised signified that Israel was then prevailing.

This tells us that at no time are we to trust in anything other than the Lord, who alone can give total and complete victory. Looking to Him brings victory, while looking to other things always brings defeat. We look to Him by exhibiting faith in Christ and His finished work.

THE CONFLICT WITH THE FLESH

This which we are discussing, and I speak of victory over the flesh, is, as we have stated, the single most important factor in the life of the believer; but yet, as important as this is, the understanding of this particular aspect of the believer's life draws a blank for most Christians. That's tragic because this particular lack of knowledge can bring about all types of problems.

Many Christians look upon regeneration, or rather their born-again experience, as a total change or renewal of the old nature, or else, they think the old nature is completely eradicated. Of course, that's like trying to overlook a 2,000-pound elephant in your living room. Perhaps one could attempt to do such a thing, but one will not be very successful, as would be obvious.

THE OLD NATURE

If, in fact, the old nature is eradicated, it would necessarily follow that the believer has nothing with which to struggle. If my old nature is taken away, and I have nothing left but the new nature, what have I to contend with? Nothing.

To all who maintain such a theory, it may be said that they seem to forget the place that Amalek occupied as it regarded this *type* in the history of the people of God. Had Israel conceived the idea that when Pharaoh's hosts were gone, their conflict was at an end, they would have been sadly put out when Amalek, in fact, came upon them. The fact is, the conflict begins after the person comes to God, just as it began for Israel after they had been delivered from Egyptian bondage.

Please note the following: Thus it is with the believer, for *"all these things happened unto them* (Israel) *for examples: and they are written for our admonition"* (I Cor. 10:11).

However, there could be no *type*, no *example*, and no *admonition* in *"these things"* for one whose old nature is made new or eradicated. Indeed, such a one can have but little need of any of these gracious provisions that God has made in His kingdom for those who are the subjects thereof.

THE OLD MAN

However, irrespective of the false assumptions of many, we are distinctly taught in the Word that the believer carries with him that which answers to Amalek, that is, *"the flesh,"* *"the old man,"* *"the carnal mind"* (Rom. 6:6; 8:7; Gal. 5:17).

If the believer doesn't understand this and doesn't know how to face them, when the problems come, and they definitely will come, he is left defenseless. In other words, he will have no vantage-ground against the enemy.

The truth is, the flesh exists in the believer and will be there until the trump sounds, or death claims us. The Holy Spirit fully recognizes this as existing, as we may easily see from various parts of the New Testament. In Romans, Chapter 6, we read, *"Let not* (the) *sin therefore 'reign' in your mortal bodies."* Such a precept would be entirely uncalled for if the flesh were not existing in the believer. It would be out of character to tell us not to let (the) sin reign if it were not actually dwelling in us. There is a great difference between *dwelling* and *reigning.* Sin dwells in a believer, but it rules and reigns in an unbeliever.

THE PRINCIPLE OF POWER

Although sin dwells in us, we have, thank God, a principle of power over it. Paul said: *"Sin shall not have dominion over you: for you are not under the law, but under grace"* (Rom. 6:14). The grace, which, by the blood of the Cross, has put away sin, ensures us the victory and gives us present power over its indwelling principle (Eph. 2:13-18).

I personally have two prayer vigils most every day. Actually, most of my praying consists of thanking the Lord for what He has done for me, as it regards the great revelation of the Cross that He has graciously afforded me, which has given me victory over the world, the flesh, and the Devil. I find myself thanking Him over and over, never dreaming that what I now have would be this wonderful.

At the very lowest time of my life, when it looked like my ministry was totally wrecked, and I was the laughingstock of the world — even as I was facing powers of darkness that I could not seem to overcome — the Spirit of the Lord spoke to me. It was a Sunday morning, and I was sitting on the platform at Family Worship Center. If I remember correctly, service had ended, and the people were praying around the altar.

All of a sudden it happened: the Spirit of God spoke to my heart and said, *"This sickness is not unto death, but for the glory of God, that the Son of God might be glorified thereby"* (Jn. 11:4).

VICTORY

To be frank with you, that Sunday morning in 1991, I didn't know the Bible nearly as well as I do now. Even though I knew that this Word recently given to me by the Lord was in the Bible, I did not know exactly where it was to be found.

As the Lord spoke that to me, the Spirit of God covered me like a glove, and I knew exactly what the Lord was saying. Even though things looked black and dim, He was telling me that the end result would not be spiritual death, but rather victory, and for the glory of God. Don't misunderstand, God never gets glory out of sin, but He definitely gets glory out of victory over sin.

As I dictate these notes on August 4, 2014, what the Lord gave to me is coming to pass, and it definitely will bring glory, even great glory, to God!

Beautifully and wondrously, He has shown me the answer to the dilemma, not only mine, but for every believer who names the name of Christ. The answer is Jesus Christ and Him crucified (I Cor. 1:23).

Little by little, the Lord has opened up to me this great path of victory. I realize that I've already related this in this volume, but I've found out the following through experience: The Message of the Cross is the simplest message there is.

However, due to the fact that Satan fights this message as he fights nothing else, it is very difficult for some believers, as simple as it might be, to grasp what is being said. So, it has to be approached from every angle and said over and over again before it finally becomes clear and plain to some believers. That's the reason we have four gospels and 14 epistles as it regards Paul.

If one inspects the four gospels and all of the epistles, even those other than Paul's, we will find that for the most part, the Holy Spirit is saying the same thing over and over, even though it is said in a little different way each time. In fact, there is a reason for all of this, but I won't take the time now to go into detail.

TRUTH

Nevertheless, irrespective as to whom the person might be, his education, or the lack thereof, if such a person, any person, will earnestly ask the Lord to reveal the truth unto him, to be sure, that person will be led to the truth. I know that for a fact.

It was 1997 that the Lord began to open up to me this great truth of the Cross. A few days after the initial inspiration, while in prayer one particular morning, the Spirit of God spoke to my heart again and said, *"The answer for which you seek is found in the Cross."*

I don't guess I will ever forget that moment. It was so simple as the Holy Spirit revealed it to me. I knew within my spirit that the Lord was giving me the answer for which I had so long sought. Then, a few days later, He revealed to me how the Holy Spirit works, which is through the faith that we have in Christ and what Christ has done for us at the Cross. To show me that, He took me to Romans 8:2.

THE REVELATION OF THE CROSS

However, this revelation just keeps expanding and is that which I believe will ever continue. When I think I've seen every room in the house, so to speak, the Lord will gently say, *"Try that door,"* and as I walk through, things are opened up that make this revelation even clearer. And everything the Lord gives me always coincides with the Scripture.

Since the revelation of the Cross, prayer has taken on a brand-new meaning. My study of the Word of God falls into the same category. The name of Jesus means far more than it ever did, with now a true understanding of that name being prevalent. It's not so much that I have learned new things, but rather that the knowledge of the Message of the Cross has put a brand-new perspective on everything, and I mean everything!

Whenever the believer is looking to heaven for leading, guidance, and sustenance, symbolized by the hands of

Moses being held high, the believer walks in victory. Whenever he starts looking to man in any capacity, symbolized by Moses letting down his hands, the enemy prevails. Our help comes from above.

LOOKING SOLELY TO THE LORD

Paul said the examples given in the Old Testament were given for our benefit (I Cor. 10:11).

The way and the manner that we look solely to the Lord is by knowing, understanding, and following the Word of God. The Word holds the answer for everything we need that *"pertain unto life and godliness"* (II Pet. 1:3).

Now please understand, the Bible tells us how to live. It's not a book of engineering, mathematics, etc.; however, what little it has to say on those subjects, to be sure, is perfectly accurate. The Bible is definitely a book of social studies; it is definitely a book regarding character; it is definitely a book regarding human interaction; and, in fact, it is the book of wisdom because it is the Word of God.

Some are fond of claiming that "all truth is God's truth." However, I remind those who claim such that truth is not a philosophy, but rather a person, in fact, the Lord Jesus Christ (Jn. 14:6).

We have what is referred to in the world of unregenerate men *subjective truth* and *objective truth*. Subjective truth is that which is subject to whatever culture there is, or whatever someone wants it to be. In fact, subjective truth is no truth at all for the simple matter that truth which is real cannot change.

OBJECTIVE TRUTH

Objective truth is that which is ordained by God and is the same the world over, irrespective of culture, climate, nationality, or whatever. When nations abandon objective truth and replace it with subjective truth, they are soon destroyed. Jesus Christ, as the living Word, is truth, which refers to the Bible as well. Jesus said, *"Your Word is truth,"* as He prayed to God the Father (Jn. 17:17). When society veers from the truth of Jesus Christ, the living Word, it has then embarked upon a lie. In fact, every single religion in the world, which refers to that which is devised by man, is, pure and simple, a lie. They contain no truth; consequently, they not only offer no help for their beleaguered followers, but rather harm.

CULTURE

As it regards culture, let's state that all culture outside of the culture of the Bible is wrong. Culture holds no place in the Word of God and in the lives of believers. When a person comes to Christ, irrespective as to whom that person might be, the color of his skin, or his nationality, he is to leave all of that which he has previously known and abide strictly by the Word of God. The Word alone is truth. To try to mix the Word of God with superstition and foolishness is an abomination!

If it is to be noticed, the Apostle Paul ministered to different nationalities and different cultures, and did so constantly. He never changed his message, irrespective of what the culture was. And yet, he had tremendous success, as should be overly obvious. Why was he successful?

He was successful because man's problem is sin, the same the world over. It doesn't matter the color of their skin, their nationality, what part of the world in which they live, who they are, or how much education they have or don't have, the problem is sin.

There's only one answer for sin, not 10, not five, not even two — just one. That answer is, *"Jesus Christ and Him crucified."*

Personally, I have also preached all over the world. I'm talking about gigantic crusades drawing up to 100,000 people a night. I've preached in Africa, the Philippines, Central America, South America, and Russia, and I never changed my message wherever we were. Besides that, I have preached by television virtually all over the world. By the grace of God, we have seen hundreds of thousands of people brought to a saving knowledge of Jesus Christ.

When we went into these places, we never changed our message simply because the message should not be changed. As stated, wherever we were, the problem was sin, and wherever we were, the solution was *"Jesus Christ and Him crucified."* The church goes wrong when it goes in other directions.

Concerning other places, I've had scores tell me, "Oh, you wouldn't go over there." When I would ask why, it would always be because of their culture.

A PERSONAL EXPERIENCE

Years ago, we were on radio all over the United States, actually, some 600 stations daily, Monday through Friday, with our daily radio program, *The Campmeeting Hour.*

There was one particular company that owned stations in various cities all over the U.S. We were on all of these stations except one. I asked the man one day why he wouldn't sell me time on that station. His answer was the usual answer: "You wouldn't go over there," etc., etc., but he finally relented and sold me time.

After about three months, he called me one day and said, "I don't understand it. We just took a poll among our audience, asking who their favorite preacher was, and you came out number one." The reason was the Spirit of God. As stated, the problem is the same, sin, and the solution is the same, *Jesus Christ and Him crucified.*

When the church begins to train its preachers (missionaries) in the realm of culture, they are missing the point altogether and will see very little, if anything, done for the Lord.

WRITTEN BY AN AFRICAN AMERICAN

The following is an article written by an African American by the name of Thomas Sowell. Even though it has nothing to do with the Word of God, at least outwardly, actually, in a sense, it does. Written by a black man, it ties in with what

I've just said concerning culture. The title that I will now give is his, and the headings that follow will be mine.

SUCCESS OF *ROOTS* REALLY WAS A TRAGEDY

Roots was the only book I knew my teenage son to read, aside from assigned school books, computer manuals, and chess books. He was thrilled to receive a copy autographed by Alex Haley, courtesy of George Haley, his brother, whom I had met (Alex Haley wrote *Roots*).

ALEX HALEY

I never really met Alex Haley, though I saw him once because we went to the same barber in Los Angeles. Then in his television appearances, Haley seemed like a very decent man. That is why it is especially painful to have to recognize now that the television series based on *Roots* is being rerun on its 25th anniversary, that its enormous success a quarter of a century ago was a tragedy for black people and for American society in general.

TRAGEDY?

Why a tragedy? The short answer is what Winston Churchill said during World War II: "If the past sits in judgment on the present, the future will be lost." Some disastrous policies had been followed in the years leading to World War II, and Churchill sharply criticized those policies at the time, but now that the war was on, looking back could only interfere with this life-and-death job at hand.

There are some very big jobs at hand for black America — and looking back at centuries past is a costly distraction from the work that needs to be done. The past that people are looking back at in *Roots* is not a wholly real past. When challenged by professional historians, Haley called his work "faction" — part fact, and part fiction. He said he had tried to give his people some myths to live by.

It was not that *Roots* merely got some details wrong. It presented some crucially false pictures that continue to dominate thinking today.

SUBJECTIVE TRUTH

Roots has a white man leading a slave raid in West Africa, where the hero Kunta Kinte was captured, looking bewildered at the chains put on him as he was led away in bondage. The village elders likewise were bewildered as to what these white men were doing, carrying their people away. In reality, West Africa was a center of slave trading before the first white man arrived there — and slavery continues in parts of it to this very moment.

Africans sold vast numbers of other Africans to Europeans. But they hardly let Europeans run around in their territory, catching people willy-nilly.

Because of the false picture of history presented by *Roots* and other sources, last year we had the farce of the President of Nigeria making demands on the United States because of the enslavement of people whom his own countrymen had enslaved, and on behalf of a country where slavery still persists, more than a century after emancipation occurred throughout the Western World.

SLAVERY

Roots also feeds the gross misconception that slavery was about white people enslaving black people. The tragedy of slavery was of far greater magnitude than that. People of every race and color were both slaves and enslavers, for thousands of years, all around the world. Europeans enslaved other Europeans for centuries before the first African was brought across the Atlantic. Asians enslaved other Asians, as well as whatever Europeans they could seize. Slavery existed in the Western hemisphere before Columbus got here.

Slavery, like cancer, was not limited to a particular country or race. To talk about cancer as if it were an American disease, or a white or black disease, would be absurd. If reparations were to be paid for slavery, everybody would owe everybody.

There is no danger of that happening. The danger is that too many black people, especially among the young and the ill-educated, will back into the third millennium still looking back at centuries past — or at fictions about centuries past — when opportunities are all around.

The ancestors of black Americans were not taken from some Eden, and there is no Eden for black Americans to return to today. If compensation were to be paid for the difference between where they are and where their ancestors came from, they would owe money, and not receive money. But it would be ridiculous to lose the future because of the past.

THE STONE

"But Moses' hands were heavy; and they took a stone, and put it under him, and he sat thereon; and Aaron and Hur stayed up his hands, the one on the one side, and the other on the other side; and his hands were steady until the going down of the sun" (Ex. 17:12).

One writer suggested that Moses was holding the rod of God up high with one hand, and when that arm grew tired, he would transfer it to the other hand; or perhaps, he was holding up the rod with both hands, spreading it out above his head.

At any rate, he soon learned that his personal endurance was limited, and so the following was done: They gave him a stone to sit on, which, as well, was symbolic of Christ.

Moses sitting on the stone portrays the fact that our own efforts soon result in spiritual exhaustion, but once we are in God's glorious way, the victory is ours.

Aaron, who was also a type of Christ as our Great High Priest, was on one side of Moses holding up his hand, and Hur was on the other side doing the same thing. Hur's name means *"light,"* which speaks to us of the Holy Spirit. The Scripture says, *"And his hands were steady until the going down of the sun."*

GOD'S WAY

God has a way, and if, as believers, we subscribe to something else other than that way, to be sure, we will bring upon ourselves much difficulty. This is the most serious business in the world. It is so serious that God had to send His only begotten Son down to this world to die on a cruel Cross in order for this problem to be properly addressed, to put it lightly.

It's about the same as an individual walking among high-powered, electrical lines, which, if touched, will bring death, or at least very serious injury. If we walk strictly on the path laid out between these high-voltage lines and don't veer from the protected way, everything will be fine; otherwise, the end result won't be good, as would be obvious.

It is the same with living this life and trying to do so without God.

The tragedy is, millions know the Lord, have accepted Him as Saviour, and are truly born again; however, even though they have trusted Christ properly for salvation, they are not at all properly trusting Him for sanctification, i.e., *the manner in which we are to live this life.*

That's the major problem for many Christians. They simply don't know how to live for God.

Just because they are believers, it doesn't make them immune to the results of a wrong direction.

DECEPTION

When I *speak of deception, perhaps it would be better to label it as "self-deception."* In other words, the individual deceives himself.

Why?

How?

The reasons are probably as varied as the individuals involved. The most hurtful thing of all is to see Christians be presented with the Message of the Cross, for that alone is the answer, and for them to show no interest, or else, even reject outright that which they hear. I know the end result is not going to be pleasant. In other words, they have just bought for themselves untold sorrow, heartache, and difficulties. In fact, they could lose their souls, and in reality, some will lose their souls.

THE WORD OF GOD

"And Joshua discomfited Amalek and his people with the edge of the sword" (Ex. 17:13).

The sword here is a type of the Word of God (Eph. 6:17).

The Word of God holds the answer to every single problem we might have, at least that which pertains to life and godliness (II Pet. 1:3-4). It's when we step outside of the Word and try to find help that we run into grievous problems. If problems that pertain to living seem to be persistent, we must come to the conclusion that our understanding of the Word is deficient in some manner. If we understand the Word and abide by the Word, which we can only do by having a proper understanding of the Cross, we will then reap the results of the Word, which is the victory it promises and the victory it delivers. Many are trying to use the Word without a proper understanding of the Cross. In some way, their understanding is going to be skewed, which will bring upon them tremendous difficulties (I Cor. 1:17; Gal. 6:14).

THE BIBLE

"And the LORD *said unto Moses, Write this for a memorial in a book, and rehearse it in the ears of Joshua: for I will utterly put out the remembrance of Amalek from under heaven"* (Ex. 17:14).

The original has, *"Write this in the book."* It is clear that a book already existed in which Moses evidently entered events of interest, and now he was divinely commanded to record in it the great victory over Amalek and the threat uttered against them.

This was the book given to Joshua; to Solomon (I Ki. 2:1-4); and to Joash (II Chron. 23:11). It was the book found by Hilkiah (II Ki., Chpt. 22), and later on, obeyed by Nehemiah

(Chpts. 8, 13). It was declared by Malachi (Chpt. 4) to have been given to Moses, used by the Lord in preaching and teaching (Lk. 24:27-44), and declared by Him to be God's Word (Mk. 7:10, 13).

It is remarkable that the first mention of the Bible should be in connection with the hostility of the natural man (Amalek) to the spiritual man (Israel). War has ever since accompanied the Book. The pagans, the papists, the skeptics, and the critics have all warred against it. No book has been so hated and so loved.

As a nation, Amalek was ultimately blotted out, just as the Lord said he would be. In Hezekiah's day, the sons of Simeon attacked *"the remnant of the Amalekites that had escaped"* and took their stronghold in Mount Seir (I Chron. 4:43). Thus, these people came to an end exactly as predicted by the Lord!

THE SPIRITUAL VICTORY

The Lord promises here total and complete victory over the flesh — of which Amalek was a type — that is, if the believer will follow the pattern of the Cross.

Even as I dictate these notes, there are untold numbers of Christians who do not understand or know the pattern of victory laid out for them by the Lord. Consequently, despite all of their best efforts otherwise, they are living a life of spiritual failure in some manner. Untold numbers of times, they have wondered, "Does it have to be this way?"

No, it doesn't have to be that way. There is victory for every believer if they will only follow God's pattern of the finished work of Christ.

THE ALTAR

"And Moses built an altar, and called the name of it Jehovah-nissi" (Ex. 17:15).

The altar symbolizes the fact that the entire legacy of Israel is built upon the Cross of Calvary. *Jehovah-nissi* means, "The Lord is my banner."

This banner was most certainly a victory banner. In fact, there is some small evidence that on this flag or banner was inscribed the posture of a rampant lion, in other words, a lion ready to pounce.

Concerning Christ, the Scripture says that *"He shall set up an ensign for the nations, and shall assemble the outcasts of Israel, and gather together the dispersed of Judah from the four corners of the earth"* (Isa. 11:12).

This could very well be the same type of banner raised by Moses and referred to as *Jehovah-nissi*. Also, Christ is called *"the Lion of the tribe of Judah"* (Rev. 5:5).

This we do know: Whatever was inscribed on this banner, it was a war banner. It signified the first victory over the flesh, with Amalek serving as the type, and it will perhaps serve as the last banner that will fly, which will take place in the coming kingdom age when Christ rules and reigns.

WAR

"For he said, Because the LORD *has sworn that the* LORD *will have war with Amalek from generation to generation"* (Ex. 17:16).

The problem of the flesh is incumbent upon every generation. The victory that I have now, while sufficient for me, will not be sufficient for my son, his son, etc. Every believer must take to himself by faith that which has been done by Christ for us and, in effect, have his own experience with the Lord in this regard.

While this conflict has been fought and won, it still must be addressed, not only by every generation, but also by every individual in each particular generation, at least those who call upon the name of Christ. Victory is found in Christ, and victory is found alone in Christ! (Rom. 6:1-14; 8:1-11; Col. 2:10-15).

> *Behold the Man of Galilee,*
> *Thorn-crown'd He hangs upon the tree;*
> *Knowing the depths of agony,*
> *To save me from my sins.*
>
> *See how His flesh by nails is torn,*
> *Each wound the mark of hate and scorn;*
> *Yet freely shame and debt is borne,*
> *To save me from my sins.*

The veil is rent, dark grows the skies,
'Tis finished!' Loud the Saviour cries;
And heaven itself weeps as He dies,
To save me from my sins.

O Saviour, when I view Your Cross,
All earthly gain I count but loss;
Take Thou my heart, purge out the dross,
And save me from my sins.

BIBLIOGRAPHY

CHAPTER 1

Arthur W. Pink, *Gleanings in Exodus*, Sovereign Grace Publishers, Lafayette, 2002, Pg. 179.

H. D. M. Spence, *The Pulpit Commentary: Exodus 15:20*, Grand Rapids, Eerdmans Publishing Company, 1978.

CHAPTER 2

Arthur W. Pink, *Gleanings in Exodus*, Sovereign Grace Publishers, Lafayette, 2002, Pg. 124.

Ibid., Pg. 131.

Ibid., Pg. 253.

CHAPTER 3

H. D. M. Spence, *The Pulpit Commentary: Exodus 17:4*, Grand Rapids, Eerdmans Publishing Company, 1978.

ABOUT EVANGELIST JIMMY SWAGGART

The Rev. Jimmy Swaggart is a Pentecostal evangelist whose anointed preaching and teaching has drawn multitudes to the Cross of Christ since 1955.

As an author, he has written more than 50 books, commentaries, study guides, and The Expositor's Study Bible, which has sold nearly 2 million copies.

As an award-winning musician and singer, Brother Swaggart has recorded more than 50 gospel albums and sold nearly 16 million recordings worldwide.

For nearly six decades, Brother Swaggart has channeled his preaching and music ministry through multiple media venues including print, radio, television and the Internet.

In 2010, Jimmy Swaggart Ministries launched its own cable channel, SonLife Broadcasting Network, which airs 24 hours a day to a potential viewing audience of more than 1 billion people around the globe.

Brother Swaggart also pastors Family Worship Center in Baton Rouge, Louisiana, the church home and headquarters of Jimmy Swaggart Ministries.

Jimmy Swaggart Ministries materials can be found at **www.jsm.org**.

NOTES

NOTES